# Gays and Lesbians

Kate Burns, *Book Editor*

Bruce Glassman, *Vice President*
Bonnie Szumski, *Publisher*
Helen Cothran, *Managing Editor*
David M. Haugen, *Series Editor*

Contemporary Issues
Companion

**GREENHAVEN PRESS**
*An imprint of Thomson Gale, a part of The Thomson Corporation*

THOMSON

GALE

Detroit • New York • San Francisco • San Diego • New Haven, Conn.
Waterville, Maine • London • Munich

*For more information, contact*
Greenhaven Press
27500 Drake Rd.
Farmington Hills, MI 48331-3535
Or you can visit our Internet site at http://www.gale.com

**LIBRARY OF CONGRESS CATALOGING-IN-PUBLICATION DATA**

Gays and lesbians / Kate Burns, book editor.
    p. cm. — (Contemporary issues companion)
Includes bibliographical references and index.
ISBN 0-7377-2456-0 (lib. : alk. paper) — ISBN 0-7377-2457-9 (pbk. : alk. paper)
    1. Gays—United States. 2. Lesbians—United States. 3. Homosexuality—United
States. 4. Gay rights—United States. 5. Gay parents—United States.
6. Homophobia—United States. I. Burns, Kate, 1969– . II. Series.
HQ76.3.U5G3945  2005
306.76'6'0973—dc22
                                                                    2004060596

# CONTENTS

# FOREWORD

In the news, on the streets, and in neighborhoods, individuals are confronted with a variety of social problems. Such problems may affect people directly: A young woman may struggle with depression, suspect a friend of having bulimia, or watch a loved one battle cancer. And even the issues that do not directly affect her private life—such as religious cults, domestic violence, or legalized gambling—still impact the larger society in which she lives. Discovering and analyzing the complexities of issues that encompass communal and societal realms as well as the world of personal experience is a valuable educational goal in the modern world.

Effectively addressing social problems requires familiarity with a constantly changing stream of data. Becoming well informed about today's controversies is an intricate process that often involves reading myriad primary and secondary sources, analyzing political debates, weighing various experts' opinions—even listening to first-hand accounts of those directly affected by the issue. For students and general observers, this can be a daunting task because of the sheer volume of information available in books, periodicals, on the evening news, and on the Internet. Researching the consequences of legalized gambling, for example, might entail sifting through congressional testimony on gambling's societal effects, examining private studies on Indian gaming, perusing numerous websites devoted to Internet betting, and reading essays written by lottery winners as well as interviews with recovering compulsive gamblers. Obtaining valuable information can be time-consuming—since it often requires researchers to pore over numerous documents and commentaries before discovering a source relevant to their particular investigation.

Greenhaven's Contemporary Issues Companion series seeks to assist this process of research by providing readers with useful and pertinent information about today's complex issues. Each volume in this anthology series focuses on a topic of current interest, presenting informative and thought-provoking selections written from a wide variety of viewpoints. The readings selected by the editors include such diverse sources as personal accounts and case studies, pertinent factual and statistical articles, and relevant commentaries and overviews. This diversity of sources and views, found in every Contemporary Issues Companion, offers readers a broad perspective in one convenient volume.

In addition, each title in the Contemporary Issues Companion series is designed especially for young adults. The selections included in every volume are chosen for their accessibility and are expertly edited in consideration of both the reading and comprehension levels of the audience. The structure of the anthologies also enhances accessibility. An introductory essay places each issue in context and provides helpful facts such as historical background or current statistics and legislation that pertain to the topic. The chapters that follow organize the material and focus on specific aspects of the book's topic. Every essay is introduced by a brief summary of its main points and biographical information about the author. These summaries aid in comprehension and can also serve to direct readers to material of immediate interest and need. Finally, a comprehensive index allows readers to efficiently scan and locate content.

The Contemporary Issues Companion series is an ideal launching point for research on a particular topic. Each anthology in the series is composed of readings taken from an extensive gamut of resources, including periodicals, newspapers, books, government documents, the publications of private and public organizations, and Internet websites. In these volumes, readers will find factual support suitable for use in reports, debates, speeches, and research papers. The anthologies also facilitate further research, featuring a book and periodical bibliography and a list of organizations to contact for additional information.

A perfect resource for both students and the general reader, Greenhaven's Contemporary Issues Companion series is sure to be a valued source of current, readable information on social problems that interest young adults. It is the editors' hope that readers will find the Contemporary Issues Companion series useful as a starting point to formulate their own opinions about and answers to the complex issues of the present day.

# INTRODUCTION

On February 26, 2004, editorial cartoonist Chris Britt published an image that was reproduced in over one hundred American newspapers. In his cartoon, President George W. Bush sits at his Oval Office desk, an American flag displayed prominently behind him. Grinning, the president holds a copy of the United States Constitution. Under the famous preamble "We the People of the United States . . . ," Bush has scribbled "EXCEPT GAYS." The words are underlined three times for emphasis.

The syndicated cartoon appeared during a period of heated debate over whether Congress should pass the federal marriage amendment (FMA), a revision to the Constitution that would ban gay marriage in every state in the union. Introduced by Republican representative Marilyn Musgrave of Colorado, the legislation declares, "Marriage in the United States shall consist only of the union of a man and a woman." It was the first time in American history that a constitutional amendment had been proposed to exclude categories of people—gays and lesbians—from a civil institution. The controversy is particularly contentious because state-sanctioned marriage bestows a long list of rights and privileges on married couples.

When the U.S. Senate finally voted on the FMA on July 14, 2004, forty-eight members were in favor of the amendment and fifty were opposed. The bill was twelve votes shy of the sixty required for passage in the Senate. However, opponents of gay marriage declared that the battle was not over. The Catholic organization Knights of Columbus announced on *U.S. Newswire* that it would fight "for as long as it takes in order to ensure that marriage, defined as the union of a man and a woman, is protected in law." A chief sponsor of the amendment, Republican senator Wayne Allard of Colorado, explained, "This is a long process. Nobody on our side, I think, ever felt for a minute that this was going to be a one-shot deal and it was going to be over with at that particular point in time."

The debate over gay marriage is one of the most politicized issues related to the status of gays and lesbians in American society. As Britt illustrates in his cartoon, proponents of gay marriage see the proposed ban as a denial of homosexuals' basic rights as Americans. Opponents believe that gay marriage undermines the institution of marriage and that homosexual people receive equal protection under the law despite the constitutional amendment. Some view the debate over gay marriage as a barometer of the degree to which society has accepted gays and lesbians into the mainstream.

Since politicians, government officials, and other powerful dignitaries make a point of articulating their opinions to the American public, it is easy to learn their position on the subject of gay marriage. More difficult is the task of determining the attitudes average Americans have about homosexuality. Examining the trends in three areas of society—television viewing, voting patterns, and hate-crime activity—can provide some insight into whether gays and lesbians are gaining acceptance in mainstream America.

One way that Americans express their attitudes is by the choices they make as consumers. In the new millennium, consumers have had more opportunities than ever before to choose television programming that features homosexual themes and characters. In 2003, for example, the lineup of such shows included Bravo's *Boy Meets Boy*, AMC's *Gay Hollywood*, ABC's *It's All Relative*, and Showtime's *The L Word*. By that time, hits like *Dawson's Creek*, *Buffy the Vampire Slayer*, *ER*, and *Six Feet Under* had already included episodes about homosexual people. Each year there are more and more portrayals of homosexual themes on television.

Furthermore, mainstream viewers are tuning in. Shows like *Will & Grace* and *Queer Eye for the Straight Guy* have high viewer ratings. NBC's *Will & Grace* shattered the "pink ceiling"—the assumption made by television executives that audiences would not watch main characters who are gay—in 1998. The gay characters Will and Jack have become viewer favorites on this prime-time show, and the sitcom continues to enjoy both critical acclaim and ratings success, consistently winning Emmys and People's Choice Awards.

When *Queer Eye for the Straight Guy* debuted in July 2003, its opening show, featuring five gay men who teach a straight man the finer points of cultured living, earned the Bravo channel its second-highest rating up to that date. Journalist Ben Patrick Johnson reports that NBC, then owner of Bravo, decided to reair the premier after *Will & Grace*, creating a block of gay-themed programming on network TV for the first time. Johnson notes that *Queer Eye* "has reached beyond a core audience of gay men and is being taken in by a mass viewership." Bravo president Laura Zalaznick recognizes that *Queer Eye* put Bravo on the map. She has since authorized several spinoffs. "This show has been so successful," she says, "I would put on the Japanese or Slovenian version."

These television trends have inspired Stephen Tropiano, author of *The Prime Time Closet: A History of Gays and Lesbians on TV*, to declare that "gays and lesbians are more visible as part of mainstream society and more accepted. We're seeing a reflection of this shift on television." However, others argue that the increase in gay visibility on TV does not necessarily reflect a greater acceptance of gays and lesbians in the United States. When gay activist Kathleen Montgomery created a made-for-TV movie with a gay lead character, she was told by several major television networks that mainstream audiences would watch only if same-sex characters did not display affection openly.

Moreover, to appeal to average viewers, the networks changed the script to revolve around a heterosexual character who interacted with minor gay characters. Montgomery found that such requirements "served as a filter through which the issue of homosexuality was processed, resulting in a televised picture of gay life designed to be . . . palatable to a mass audience." Similarly, other critics have argued that gay characters on mainstream TV infrequently stretch beyond the stereotype of the young, effeminate, Caucasian man. Therefore, they point out, the diverse experiences of a sizable gay and lesbian population are largely marginalized or completely silenced. The limited representations suggest that Americans are more accepting of *some* gays on TV, but not necessarily of *all* gay and lesbian people.

Examining voting patterns is a way to gauge how Americans feel about gays and lesbians in real life rather than in fictional representations. What do voters say when gay and lesbian concerns that may affect their daily lives show up on election ballots? Several key issues have been under consideration in recent years. One of the major issues before voters is whether to open American society to gay marriage. Although the federal marriage amendment died in the U.S. Senate, legislators are proposing amendments to several state constitutions to limit marriage to heterosexual couples. By 2004, voters in two states, Missouri and Louisiana, had approved amendments to their state constitutions defining marriage as between one man and one woman. In twenty-five other states, similar proposals were pending and had yet to reach voters as of this writing. Another state, Massachusetts, granted full marriage rights to same-sex couples in 2004, and five other states established some rights for same-sex couples in domestic partnerships. However, opponents of these measures argued that many of the decisions to recognize gay couples came from activist judges rather than voters, therefore overstepping the will of mainstream America.

While the issue of gay marriage is still hotly debated, numerous Americans have decided that discrimination against gays and lesbians in the workplace is wrong. A survey of states in 2003 by the Human Rights Campaign found that voters in fourteen states had passed legislation prohibiting employers from discriminating against workers based on sexual orientation. Eleven more states had an executive or administrative order prohibiting discrimination. Moreover, the survey showed that nine states and many individual cities had a law or policy that provided gay and lesbian state employees with domestic partner benefits. For example, state employees in Connecticut can obtain health insurance for their same-sex partners, and municipal workers in Chicago can have their relationships acknowledged in a domestic partner registry.

Another way to gauge acceptance of homosexuality is to examine how Americans behave toward gay and lesbian people. Some Americans, unfortunately, express their *lack* of acceptance of homosexuality with their fists, knives, and guns. The Federal Bureau of Investigation (FBI) defines a hate crime as "a criminal offense committed against a person, property or society which is motivated, in whole or in part, by the offender's bias against a race, religion, disability, sexual orientation or ethnicity/national origin." The number of hate crimes against gays and lesbians can serve as evidence of the level of antihomosexual sentiment in a society.

In accordance with the 1990 Hate Crimes Statistics Act, the FBI began keeping a record of hate crimes classified by the race, religion, ethnicity and national origin, and sexual orientation of the victims. According to the 2002 report, there were 1,246 reported antigay hate crimes in the United States. Furthermore, hate crimes against homosexuals that year were the third-largest category of hate crimes (crimes motivated by race were the largest group, followed by crimes motivated by religious hatred). According to the FBI, reported antigay violence has been increasing since 1996, when there were 1,016 incidents recorded. Nongovernment organizations in the United States have been tracking hate crimes as well. A 2001 report by the National Coalition of Anti-Violence Programs (NCAVP) shows an increase in the amount of antigay violence between 1999 and 2000, with a total of 2,151 antigay incidents reported in 2000. The Southern Poverty Law Center notes that attacks against homosexuals tend to be more severe than those against other minority groups. It recorded, for example, that twenty-one gays and lesbians were brutally killed in 1996 because of their sexual orientation.

On the other hand, citizens in some states have organized to protest antigay hate crimes. In Roanoke, Virginia, after a man opened fire inside a gay bar, killing one patron and injuring six others in 2001, citizens raised money for the survivors' medical bills and led a prayer vigil that attracted a thousand supporters in the small community. When three teens were assaulted for being gay a year later in Somerville, Massachusetts, community members and local legislators organized to increase education and outreach to raise awareness of hate crimes in the city. Other communities in the United States have since been organizing to prevent hate crimes. Such activism indicates a growing intolerance of homophobic violence. A total of twenty-nine states have passed legislation to include sexual orientation in the categories used to collect hate crime data and persecute offenders. Some people argue that these laws show that there is now more mainstream approval for gays and lesbians; others contend that the legislation only shows that most Americans do not tolerate violence as a way to repress homosexuality.

Yet it is clear that many public opinion polls do show an increase in acceptance of gays and lesbians compared to previous years. The American Enterprise Institute, a conservative think tank in Washington, D.C., compiled the results of major public opinion polls taken over the course of thirty years, from 1973 to 2003. Its research reveals several remarkable shifts, including a 29 percent increase in public acceptance of gays in the military since 1977 and a 34 percent increase in the approval of gays as elementary school teachers since 1977. The institute also reported that 59 percent of those polled in 1999 would vote for a well-qualified presidential candidate who was gay, up from 26 percent in 1978. What seems to influence Americans to change their attitudes toward homosexuals? Manuel Mendoza of the *Dallas Morning News* reports:

> The No. 1 reason people have changed their minds? More Americans, polls show, know someone who's gay—a family member, a friend, a co-worker—because more gay men and lesbians have been coming out of the closet. "You work with people on a day-to-day basis, and they're not ogres, they're not something demonic, and it becomes more acceptable," said Edd Sewell, a communications professor at Virginia Tech.

Cheryl Jacques of the Human Rights Campaign agrees. "It all boils down to a single premise," she asserts. "It is far harder to hate and discriminate against someone you know than someone you don't know."

Determining whether gays and lesbians are accepted by the majority of Americans continues to be difficult. *Contemporary Issues Companion: Gays and Lesbians* provides insight into the key debates related to gay and lesbian issues in contemporary society. Some of the selections argue strongly for increasing the acceptance of gays and lesbians, and others just as strongly oppose greater acceptance. Several authors bring a historical perspective to bear on current controversies in order to clarify ongoing discussions about gays and lesbians in America. Providing a balance of essays, reports, and personal narratives, this volume explores homosexuality in relation to families, politics, the courts, popular culture, education, and religion.

CHAPTER 1

# GAYS AND LESBIANS IN HISTORY

Contemporary Issues
Companion

# HOW HOMOSEXUALITY BECAME STIGMATIZED

Gilbert Herdt and Bruce Koff

Homophobia, the fear or hatred of homosexuality, can be identified in several different religious and scientific belief systems in Western history. In an effort to promote procreation as the purpose for all sexual intimacy, early Christians condemned same-sex love along with other nonprocreative relationships. When science displaced religion as the esteemed cultural authority during the Enlightenment, some medical pioneers hoped to protect homosexuals from persecution by arguing that homosexuality was a biological condition rather than a moral defect. Though well intentioned, these efforts paved the way for homosexuality to be classified as medical "degeneration" or a mental "disease" during the early twentieth century. By the 1960s changing notions about sexual liberation and modern scientific research led many to challenge the stigmatization of homosexuality and inspired the gay rights movement. Gilbert Herdt and Bruce Koff summarize the history of homophobia in this excerpt from their book *Something to Tell You: The Road Families Travel When a Child Is Gay.* Herdt is the director of human sexuality studies at San Francisco State University and the author and editor of a number of books on gays and lesbians, including *Same Sex, Different Cultures: Exploring Gay and Lesbian Lives* and *Gay Culture in America.* Bruce Koff is the former executive director of Horizons Community Services, the largest social service agency for gays and lesbians in the Midwest. He is currently on the faculty of the Chicago Center for Family Health of the University of Chicago and maintains a private psychotherapy practice specializing in work with gays, lesbians, and their families.

The social history of homosexuality can be traced now due to the efforts of a new generation of historians, sociologists, and anthropologists who have discovered a complex story about same-sex relations in culture and society. As these scholars have shown, homophobia [the fear or hatred of homosexuality] evolved through the ages. Homosexuality was deemed at some points in time a sin, at other points "moral degeneracy," at others a "disease," and now, more recently, a "destructive lifestyle" or a "genetic flaw." Each classification or attribution continued to promote the stigmatization of same-sex love. But all these negative terms reflect more myth than science or moral profundity. They are the signs of a shame culture and a history that assigns blame for being lesbian or gay. The historical attempts to classify, categorize, morbidify, criminalize, and condemn love between women or love between men also reflect a culture's wish to validate a central organizing principle for all human relationships. But that principle is no longer relevant to everyone, nor is it necessary in order for society to thrive that the principle be universally followed.

The Church's aim to stigmatize homosexuality, as scholars have argued, grew out of the politics and ascetic movements of its early history and an over-riding emphasis on the promotion of procreation. With the Enlightenment, medical science began to supplant religion in Western culture. Though the Enlightenment valorized rationality, sexual deviance continued to be treated harshly, even by execution. It is within the context of scientific study and the classification of sexual differences that the identity of "the homosexual" eventually emerged, during the second half of the nineteenth century.

## Early Sexology and Psychology

Nineteenth- and early twentieth-century medical men, such as Richard von Krafft-Ebing, Havelock Ellis, and Sigmund Freud, attempted to lessen antihomosexual prejudices by explaining homosexuality as a medical rather than a moral problem. But their well-intentioned efforts were in the end very destructive. This line of thinking was to allow the Nazis, later in the twentieth century, to condemn and murder homosexuals as "diseased." And for a very long time in the twentieth century, many authorities, including those who were compassionate and did not believe that homosexuality merited imprisonment or punishment, nevertheless continued to view it as an innate sickness that required treatment.

Scientific sexology was divided over these theories in the first half of the twentieth century. Freud, for instance, early in his career, developed a "degeneration" theory about homosexuality. More than thirty years later, however, in his famous 1935 letter to an American mother, Freud suggested that homosexuality was "no vice, no degradation [and] cannot be classified as an illness." Freud argued that homosexuality, like left-handedness, could probably not be changed and should be accepted by the homosexual and his family.

However, by the 1940s a number of American psychiatrists sought to reinstate the "disease model," arguing that homosexuality was caused by bad parenting. For many years, psychoanalytic study continued to perpetuate this false idea. Homosexuality was labeled a mental illness, a point of view that flourished in mid-twentieth-century America, particularly during the 1950s when the pressure of Cold War toward conformity was at its height. The homosexual became a key target for blackmail and arrest, an object of scorn, and was even associated with communism and traitorous conduct. Raids on gay bars and even gay people's private parties were common. Scandal was frequent, since people arrested as homosexuals often had their names published in the newspapers. Mistrust was high and secrecy seemed tantamount to survival.

## New Evidence, New Ideas

It is against this backdrop that the first real challenges to heterosexual orthodoxy and homosexual secrecy emerged. First came the Kinsey Reports, which documented that homosexual behavior was far more common in the United States than had previously been believed. In addition, anthropological studies began to reveal that many societies permit the expression of same-sex desire, often in childhood and adolescence, and that some extend the approval of same-sex relations into adulthood. In the early 1950s, for example, sociologist Clelland Ford and biologist Frank Beach showed that sexual practice varied enormously across a sample of many societies around the world. Homosexual practice was approved and permitted for some persons in more than 60 percent of the groups they surveyed. Shortly thereafter, the great American psychologist Evelyn Hooker offered a critique of existing research on homosexuality as a disease. Hooker interviewed numerous self-identified homosexual men and showed that homosexuals who were not in clinical treatment for emotional problems had no greater incidence of psychological impairment or disturbed relations than their heterosexual counterparts. She also suggested that the stigmatizing of homosexuality was far more harmful to the psychological well-being of gay men than any aspect of homosexuality itself.

In addition, with the introduction of widespread birth control and the emergence of the sexual liberation movement in the 1960s, the absolute link between sex and procreation was broken. If sex between a man and a woman could be viewed primarily as a form of human expression and source of pleasure rather than being exclusively the means to reproduction of the species, then justice demanded that the prejudice against same-sex relationships be questioned. The civil rights struggles and the women's liberation movement in the 1960s also influenced a new and more humanistic psychology that looked seriously at the problems of power, oppression, discrimination, and abuse in society. Gays and lesbians in the 1960s and 1970s increasingly came to see themselves as an oppressed group and began to challenge actively the notion of homosexuality as a mental illness, a sin, or a crime.

## Challenging Discrimination

The famous Stonewall Inn riots in New York in 1969, now celebrated every June through the commemoration of the Gay and Lesbian Pride Day Parade, was a watershed. The riots took place on a sultry summer evening, when a typical police raid on a homosexual tavern did not lead to the usual intimidation or slinking away: instead, homosexuals fought back. The Stonewall riots marked the symbolic beginning of a long movement to end discrimination based upon sexual orientation.

A new American culture-formation of individual development began to distinguish between the identity constructs of "homosexual" and those of "gay" or "lesbian." The gay and lesbian rights movement largely rejected the term "homosexual," which was created in the nineteenth century under the influence of the disease model and (1970s militants argued) resulted in feelings of secrecy and shame. The terms "gay" and "lesbian" were more widely adopted and fostered pride and dignity. David Leavitt's novel *The Lost Language of Cranes* eloquently captures the difference between the pre- and post-Stonewall generations. Leavitt presents a closeted homosexual father, who fears the shame of his desires and blames himself for the failure of his marriage, and his openly gay son, who takes pride in his aspirations, including the desire to have a lover and be open to his parents.

Sweeping cultural change and more empirically sound research soon made it apparent that the notion of homosexuality as "illness" has no basis in science, and that the notion's only purpose was to perpetuate stigmatizing myths. In 1974 the American Psychiatric Association officially declassified homosexuality as a mental illness. Since then scholars and mental health professionals have, by-and-large, understood lesbian and gay lifeways as alternative paths of human development. Many religious groups are trying to overcome homosexuality's stigmatized history in a variety of ways, such as the sanctioning of same-sex marriage and the ordination of gay and lesbian clergy. In spite of this progress, however, discrimination against homosexuals remains legal in many places in the land. Indeed, about twenty states of the United States continue to sanction "sodomy" laws and other forms of legal prohibition of homosexuality.[1]

## Effects of Shame-Based Thinking on Families

In light of the history of homophobia, it is perhaps easy to understand why the vestiges of what we call the "shame-based" approaches to homosexuality continue to permeate our culture in general, and

---

1. As of publication of this book, the U.S. Supreme Court invalidated the criminal prohibition of homosexual sodomy in the *Lawrence v. Texas* landmark case.

the thinking of many parents in particular. In her book, *Parents Matter*, Ann Muller speaks cogently of the shame that many parents still feel upon hearing the news that their child is gay. She has tried to analyze why parents often feel blamed—by society, by their families, and by themselves. Her insight reminds us of the negative effects of antiquated notions about homosexuality on parents who are grappling with accepting the news of their child's sexual orientation:

> The pathologic view of parents as the cause of homosexuality is still widely believed. Freud's dominant mother and weak father have become a pervasive part of our culture, the trolls of psychiatry. The very imprecision of the Freudian and neo-Freudian categories of parental guilt encourages their continued application. The theory allows the unsophisticated to feel smug, to play doctor. It makes the parents of young children nervous and self-conscious. How much love is enough love? It allows lesbian daughters and gay sons to blame their parents. It creates massive guilt, emotional pain, and self-imposed isolation from parents.

The "reparative therapy" approaches, which claim to convert homosexual people into heterosexuals, represent another attempt of pseudoscience, under the cloak of medical authority, to demean lesbians, gay men, and their families. As researcher Timothy Murphy concludes in his review of attempts to redirect sexual orientation, "there would be no reorientation techniques where there was no interpretation that homoeroticism is an inferior state." Clearly the heroic struggle that parents and their gay and lesbian children face is to confront these remnants of an earlier era, acknowledge their destructive impact, and develop a new set of cultural ideals more suitable to the reality of who they are and what they require to build meaningful lives.

# THE NATIVE AMERICAN TRADITION OF ACCEPTANCE

Androphile Project

Before Europeans traveled across the ocean and made contact with Native Americans, most tribal societies accepted homosexual members. Seen as people with a distinct gender identity, such "two-spirit" members often performed the work of both men and women and had relationships with same-sex partners. Moreover, in many tribes, such as the Dinéh (Navajo), Mohave, and Lakota (Sioux), two-spirit people were highly respected and believed to possess special spiritual powers. The following selection from the Androphile Project explains that European contact influenced the decline of Native Americans' reverence for two-spirit people, replacing veneration with traditional European views that homosexuality is sinful and repulsive. However, some contemporary Native American gays and lesbians are leading a revival of the respected two-spirit tradition in their families and tribes. The Androphile Project is a research Web site that offers information about love between men throughout history in many different cultures around the world.

The popular take on "how the West was won" evokes images of rowdy cowboys and brave Indians slugging it out, with the noble but obsolete Indians gradually falling back and fading away before the military might of the Europeans, and the moral force of "manifest destiny," the principle that the white American has a God-given mandate to conquer and rule the entire temperate zone of North America from the Atlantic to the Pacific coast. All the while the Indian is seen as faithfully paired off with his "squaw," and the cowboy or the soldier as getting his rocks off on the run in the local bordello, under the tough but benign gaze of the hard-nosed madam: "Wham, bam, thank you m'am!"

Whatever may be the merits of that colonial mentality, still prevalent *de facto* [in fact] and *de jure* [by law] throughout the U.S., the fact is that this image has little to do with how either the victor or the vanquished lived. But only a handful of scholars are likely to be aware of the rich veins of homoerotic tradition pervading the culture of the invaders as well as that of the First Nations whose lands they barged through. Of the intimate friendships and love affairs among cowboys we will have little to say here. And of the furtive kisses between soldiers, [poet] Walt Whitman has already said a great deal.

## Two-Spirit Identity

For the moment the ancient patterns of male love woven through the fiber of almost every (yes, variety allowed even for the occasional homophobic tribe) Native culture on the American continent is of greater interest. The many forms of this tradition have until recently been lumped by historians under the rubric of berdachism, "berdache" being defined by Webster's Dictionary as a "homosexual male—an American Indian transvestite assuming more or less permanently the dress, social status, and role of a woman."

Not surprisingly, the experience of Native peoples is something other than either the popular or the professional stereotype. Though it would be presumptuous to claim to represent its essence from the perspective of an outsider, we can still look at certain features of two-spirit [berdache] life in Native cultures, features that delineate how First Nations peoples integrated individuals with uncommon gender identity into their society.

The first step on the path to a two-spirit life was taken during childhood. The Papago ritual is representative of this early integration: If parents noticed that a son was disinterested in boyish play or manly work they would set up a ceremony to determine which way the boy would be brought up. They would make an enclosure of brush, and place in the center both a man's bow and a woman's basket. The boy was told to go inside the circle of brush and to bring something out, and as he entered the brush would be set on fire. [As anthropologist Ruth Underhill reports] "They watched what he took with him as he ran out, and if it was the basketry materials they reconciled themselves to his being a berdache."

The Mohave ritual, usually carried out when the child is between the ages of nine and twelve, has a different form, but keeps the central element of allowing the child's nature to manifest itself: A singing circle is prepared, unbeknownst to the boy, involving the whole community as well as distant friends and relatives. On the day of the ceremony everyone gathers round and the boy is led into the middle of the circle. If he remains there, the singer, hidden in the crowd, begins to sing the ritual songs and the boy, if he is destined to follow the two-spirit road, starts to dance in the fashion of a woman. "He cannot help it," say the Mohave. After the fourth song the boy is declared to be a two-spirit person and is raised from then on in the appropriate manner, [reports scientist George Devereaux].

## Two-Spirit Tribal Life

What manner was that? It consisted of teaching the young boy to do women's work as well as that reserved for men. He would also spend time with healers, often two-spirit people themselves. Above all, his childhood was marked by acceptance and understanding. That did not necessarily insulate the boy from being ribbed about his 'otherness.' Joseph Quinones, the cousin of a Yaqui two-spirit youth, relates that: "One time we kids got down on him for not being typically masculine, but my Great Aunt, who is the clan matriarch, came down on us real strongly. She said it was part of his character and we should respect him."

In recent times that pattern of acceptance has been undermined by the boarding school education forced upon Native children, by the influence of Christian missionaries, and increasingly by the encroachment of television into the psychic space of the tribe, with the result that two-spirit people are more and more being viewed with suspicion by the less traditionalist in their community. [Scholar] Robert Stoller observes the ". . . deterioration in American Indians of techniques for ritualizing cross-gender behavior. No longer is a place provided for the role—more, the identity—of a male-woman, the dimensions of which are fixed by customs, rules, tradeoffs and responsibilities. The tribes have forgotten. Instead, this role appears as a ghost."

All tribes were aware of the existence of two-spirit people, and each still has a name for them. The Dinéh (Navaho) refer to them as *nàdleehé* one who is 'transformed', the Lakota (Sioux) as *winkte*, the Mohave as a *alyha*, the Zuni as *lhamana*, the Omaha as *mexoga*, the Aleut and Kodiak as *achnucek*, the Zapotec as *ira' muxe*, the Cheyenne as *he man eh*. This abundance of terms testifies to the familiarity of Native Americans with gender-variant people. For proof of the sacred role they held, and hold, in Native society we again turn to Native sources. Terry Calling Eagle, a Lakota man, recounts: "Winktes have to be born that way. People know that a person is going to become a winkte very early in his life. At about age twelve parents will take him to a ceremony to communicate with past winktes who had power, to verify if it is just a phase or a permanent thing for his lifetime. If the proper vision takes place, and communication with a past winkte is established, then everybody accepts him as a winkte."

Claire R. Farrer, an anthropologist who has "gone native" in the best sense of the term, reports on the present situation among the Mescalero Apache: "Multigendered adult people at Mescalero are usually presumed to be people of power. Because they have both maleness and femaleness totally entwined in one body, they are known to be able to 'see' with the eyes of both proper men and proper women. They are often called upon to be healers, or mediators, or interpreters of dreams, or expected to become singers or others whose lives are devoted to the welfare of the group. If they do extraordinary things in any aspect of life, it is assumed that they have the license and power to do so and, therefore, they are not questioned."

In everyday life the two-spirit male typically would wear women's clothes and do women's work. He would be accepted as "one of the girls." He might take a husband from among the men of the tribe, or might have affairs with several, or both. Generally two-spirit males were not expected to have sexual relations with women. None of these "rules" however were ironbound. Again and again we see that variation from the norm, change, transformation, and fluidity of roles for those who felt called to that path was welcomed and appreciated. Here we have to confront a very real epistemological problem: it is impossible to define precisely what two-spirit experience is. Though all agree such individuals exist, [says anthropologist Carolyn Epple,] "the particulars of that identity remain variable." We may have to content ourselves with the explanation offered by P.K., one of Epple's Dinéh teachers, who said that we need to ". . . see nàdleehé as human beings responding to situations."

Besides their spiritual abilities, their capacity for work also figured into the high status of two-spirit people. Even though a two-spirit male would have taken on the gender identity of a woman, he would still have the endurance and strength of a man. Thus his productivity was greater than that of most women, and for that reason also he would have been valued as a marriage partner. Other characteristics that Natives associate with two-spirit people and that help explain their desirability as partners are a highly developed ability to relate to and teach children, a generous nature, and exceptional intellectual and artistic skills.

## Contemporary Native Gays and Lesbians

As mentioned before, many of the ancient two-spirit ways are no longer being practiced. Nonetheless Native two-spirit peoples are experiencing a re-awakening to the validity, and to the cultural and spiritual roots, of their inner calling. Many who, as a result of the cultural scorched-earth policies of the Bureau of Indian Affairs, had sought escape from isolation and rejection by adopting modern "gay" identities are now reconnecting with their heritage by way of groups like the Native Gay and Lesbian Gathering. They are re-interpreting their identity in terms dictated neither by white culture nor by ancient customs, or perhaps by both. The result is a mix peculiarly their own, which by breaking with both traditional as well as modern forms remains true to the essence of the two-spirit life. As [writer] Michael Red Earth tells it: "In today's world it is easy to become confused by titles: gay, straight, bi, winkte or queer. For me, once I realized that my family was responding to me and interacting with me with respect and acceptance, and once I realized that this respect and acceptance was a legacy of our traditional Native past, I was empowered to present my whole self to the world and reassume the responsibilities of being a two-spirited person."

Though . . . the discussion so far has been limited to the male experience in Native American societies, this should not be construed to mean that the two-spirit path was, or is, closed to women. If any conclusion can be drawn from what we know about gender variation in traditional Native society it is that gender flexibility in any individual is welcomed as a rare and precious aspect of human experience, a special talent to live life in a fresh, spontaneously authentic way that enriches and empowers the lives of all in the community. It is a lasting testament to the psychological sophistication of Native tribes that they recognized two-spirit people as being engines of creativity, change and innovation (much as they have been in other cultures and continue to be in ours) and co-operated in creating the sacred space in which such people could manifest. As Joe Medicine Crow, a Crow traditionalist, told [writer] Walter Williams, "We don't waste people the way white society does. Every person has their gift."

# THE GAY AND LESBIAN RIGHTS MOVEMENT IN THE UNITED STATES

Stephen Engel

During World War II, previously isolated gays and lesbians who joined the military had the opportunity to discover other people who considered themselves to be homosexual. As Stephen Engel explains, this created a new sense of community for American gays and lesbians. Shortly after the war, "homophile" organizations, most notably the Mattachine Society and the Daughters of Bilitis, emerged to support the idea of homosexuals as a minority group that deserved basic human rights and respect. In the 1970s the first full-fledged gay liberation movement began, modeling itself after other liberation movements of the era, including the antiwar, black power, and feminist movements. Debates over political strategies among activists, growing acceptance in the mainstream culture, and the specter of AIDS had both unifying and splintering effects on the gay rights movement of the 1980s and 1990s. In the new millennium, the movement has attained remarkable visibility in the public arena, yet Engel argues that political complacency among many gays and increasing disharmony among various segments of the movement limit the political power and liberation of gays and lesbians in America today. Engel is the author of *The Unfinished Revolution: Social Movement Theory and the Gay and Lesbian Movement*.

The emergence of the gay and lesbian movement in the United States is often pinpointed to an exact date and time: 1:20 A.M. on Saturday, 28 June 1969. On this day, police officers raided a well-known gay bar, the Stonewall Inn, on Christopher Street in Greenwich Village. The police raid was not uncommon; however, the reaction of the patrons was extraordinary: they fought back, sparking two days and nights of riotous confrontation between approximately four hundred New York police officers and two thousand gay men and women, especially people of color. This event is so crucial because it signifies the emer-

Stephen Engel, "Making a Minority: Understanding the Formation of the Gay and Lesbian Movement in the United States," *Handbook of Lesbian and Gay Studies*, edited by Diane Richardson and Steven Seidman. Thousand Oaks, CA: Sage, 2002. Copyright © 2002 by Sage Publications, Ltd. Reproduced by permission.

gence of group action among a previously docile, invisible, and seemingly powerless minority. Soon after the riots, various organizations including the Gay Liberation Front (GLF) were created to mobilize gay men and lesbians into a viable political force. As historian John D'Emilio notes, a curious contradiction developed between GLF rhetoric and the reality of the homosexual community. Activists of the early 1970s denounced the invisibility and silence that many felt characterized the homosexual lifestyle. However, leaders of liberation movement organizations demonstrated an uncanny ability to mobilize these supposedly silent and isolated masses: by the middle of the 1970s over one thousand gay and lesbian organizations existed in the United States. This apparent inconsistency can be resolved if we take D'Emilio's advice: 'clearly what the movement achieved and how lesbians and gay men responded to it belied the rhetoric of isolation and invisibility. Isolated men and women do not create, almost overnight, a mass movement premised upon a shared group identity.' In other words, the gay and lesbian movement did not suddenly start at a given hour on a certain day following a specific event; rather, it embodies an historical process marked by diverse opportunities, multiple organizational networks, and instances, such as the Stonewall riots, which ushered in a shift in the personal perspectives of gay men and lesbians themselves.

## World War II

D'Emilio suggests that the first significant opportunity for homosexual identity formation was World War II. The altered social conditions of the war, i.e., a sex-segregated society marked both by soldiers under the strain of warfare and a large influx of women into the domestic labor force, provided a critical opportunity for gay men and lesbians to come into contact with one another. The sex-segregated atmosphere created by militarization immensely disrupted the heterosexual patterns of peacetime life; this phenomenon is no more apparent than in the armed forces. First, by asking recruits if they had ever felt any erotic attraction for members of the same sex, the military was rupturing the silence that shrouded a tabooed behavior, some times introducing men to the concept for the first time. Second, the war brought previously isolated homosexuals together. Given that the recruits could merely lie about their sexual inclinations and that the draft preferred young and single men, it was likely that the armed forces would contain a disproportionately high percentage of gay men relative to civilian society. Third, heterosexual men sometimes engaged in 'situational homosexuality' to attain a level of physical intimacy deprived by the war experience. It was not uncommon for men to dance together at canteens, to share beds at hotels when on leave, or to share train berths while in transit. The critical point is not that the war experience fostered homoerotic feelings and a rise in homosexuality.

Rather, the war's disruption of the social environment provided the *opportunity* for homosexuals to meet, to realize others like themselves existed, and to abandon the isolation that characterized the homosexual lifestyle of the pre-war period. The war created a sexual situation where individuals with homosexual feelings or tendencies could more readily explore them without the absolute fear of exposure. . . .

## The Cold War

The onset of Cold War anti-Communist panic marked the 1950s as a decade rife with political repression. Communists were not the only target; individuals who did not conform to the mainstream heteronormative image reminiscent of the pre-war period were perceived as enemies of the state. Amidst growing fears that homosexuals—one such non-conforming group—were infiltrating the highest levels of government and threatening national security, the Senate Investigations Subcommittee of the Committee on Expenditures in the Executive Department began an inquiry in June of 1950 and released its report, 'Employment of Homosexuals and Other Sex Perverts in the U.S. Government', in December of 1950. The report's attack on homosexuals was twofold: it degraded the personal character of gay men and lesbians, and it contended that homosexuals embodied a threat to national security. The report used Kinsey's conclusions regarding the higher prevalence of homosexuality than previously thought to promote a sense of paranoia: these diseased individuals were everywhere and, worse yet, they could not be detected by any physical features. The committee concluded that homosexuals exhibited emotional instability and moral weakness. According to the Senate report, employing homosexuals would not only out fellow workers at risk, but would endanger national integrity. The report's ultimate conclusion was that homosexuals were fundamentally unsuited for employment in the federal government. Between 1947 and 1950, the dismissal rate of homosexuals from an executive branch office averaged five per month. Homosexuals were officially banned from the government with the passage of Executive Order 10450 under President Eisenhower in April of 1953. In total, between 1947 and 1950, 1,700 applicants for government positions were turned away because of professed homosexuality, 4,380 individuals were discharged from military service, and 420 gay men and lesbians were dismissed or forced to resign from government posts. . . .

## The Mattachine Society

Founded by Harry Hay in April of 1951 in Los Angeles and modeled after the communist party, the Mattachine Society was the first organization of what would become the homophile movement. The secret hierarchical and cell-like structure was necessitated, according to the founders, by the oppressive environment fostered by McCarthyism.

Yet, Mattachine drew on communism for more than an organizational template; Marxist ideology laid the blueprints to mobilize a
mass homosexual constituency for political action. Adapting a Marxist understanding of class politics, Hay and the other founding members theorized that homosexuals constituted an oppressed minority
group. Homosexuals, like members of the proletariat, were trapped in
a state of false consciousness purported and defended by the heterosexual majority which maintained homosexuality to be a morally
reprehensible individual aberration. Hence, the early Mattachine attempted to promote a measure of cognitive liberation and homosexual collective identity; it advocated the development of a group consciousness similar to that of other ethnic minority groups in the
United States. Mattachine, under Hay's direction, whether intentional
or not, was capitalizing on a master frame which has had a great deal
of cultural resonance in the United States: minority demands for civil
rights. By asserting that homosexuals constituted a minority comparable to recognized ethnic groups, Mattachine defined itself rather
than being defined by the dominant culture: homosexuality was distinct from and morally equivalent to heterosexuality. Furthermore,
the comparison to ethnic minorities provided a model for action:
homosexuals should follow the lead of other groups and politically
organize for equal civil rights.

By 1953, the Mattachine Society had an estimated 2000 members
and one hundred discussion groups stretching from San Diego to
Santa Monica, California. Given the rise of McCarthyism, some members became increasingly uncomfortable with the organization's secre-
tive structure and leftist orientation. In order to mitigate growing dis-
sension, the original five members called for a convention in April of
1953 to convert the Mattachine Society into an above-ground organization. The conference exacerbated the division between moderate
and militant perspectives. Hay and the other founders were confronted
by demands that emphasized assimilation and suggested that homosexual behavior was a minor characteristic that should not create a rift
with the heterosexual majority. The growing fears about the current
leaders' communist backgrounds led to a dramatic shift in leadership.
The assimilationist tendency gained control of the organization and
steered it towards what D'Emilio calls a 'retreat to respectability'. . . .

## Daughters of Bilitis

By the end of 1955, Mattachine Society chapters were set up in San
Francisco, New York, and Chicago. On September 21, 1955, another
homophile organization, the Daughters of Bilitis (DOB), was established by four lesbian couples in San Francisco, though Del Martin
and Phyllis Lyon are credited with maintaining it in early years. This
organization, similar to the assimilationist Mattachine, emphasized
education and self-help activities. The DOB's 'Statement of Purpose'

cites as its main goals 'education of the variant, with particular emphasis on the psychological, physiological and socio-logical aspects, to enable her [the lesbian] to understand herself and make her adjustment to society in all its social, civic, and economic implications.' Despite its commitment to legal reform, stated as its final aim in its statement of purpose, the DOB functioned ultimately as a safe meeting space for lesbians and bisexual women who did not feel comfortable in the lesbian bar scene. In contrast to the early Mattachine, the DOB had no interest in collectively organizing lesbians for political action; it had no agenda to promote group identity. Its main function, like that of the latter Mattachine, was to integrate the homosexual into heterosexual society by de-emphasizing sexual difference and seeking acceptance from the majority culture.

Relative to gay men, lesbians had to navigate a dual identity that suffered a dual oppression. Lesbians were oppressed because they were lesbians, but also more generally because they were women; consequently, an internal debate erupted in many women about whether to remain active in the homophile movement through DOB or whether to defect to the women's movement through networks such as the National Organization of Women. Personifying this struggle, activist Shirley Willer, in a 1966 address to the National Planning Committee of Homophile Organizations, contended that problems such as police harassment and sodomy law, which seemed to make up the majority of the homophile agenda, did not affect women. Willer further claimed that 'there has been little evidence however, that the male homosexual has any intention of making common cause with us [lesbians]. We suspect that should the male homosexual achieve his particular objective in regard to his homosexuality he might possibly become more of an adamant foe of women's rights than the heterosexual male has been.' Such harsh comments were mitigated by Willer's simultaneous desire to maintain the DOB's participation in the homophile movement so as to at least expand the perspective of the male-dominated movement. . . .

## 1970s: Coming Out and Cognitive Liberation

What we now perceive as the lesbian, gay, bisexual, and transgender (LGBT) movement at the beginning of the twenty-first century planted its roots in the 1970s; however, the movement that took shape in that decade bears little resemblance to its modern form of various and highly organized state and national-level organizations. To conceive of a gay and lesbian rights movement in the 1970s is to confront a decentralized history of numerous short-lived organizations, clashing personalities, grassroots, local, and state-level activism, the rise of a religiously-based conservative backlash, and the curious denouement of a movement before it seemingly reached political climax. The struggle for gay and lesbian rights in the 1970s unfolded in New York City, San Francisco,

Los Angeles, Washington, DC, Miami, Boston, Minneapolis-St. Paul, Eugene, Oregon, and Wichita, Kansas. The cast of activists is wide and varied: Craig Rodwell, Jim Owles, Jim Fouratt, Marty Robinson, Frank Kameny, Elaine Noble, Harvey Milk, Virginia Apuzzo, Barbara Gittings, Rita Mae Brown, Bruce Voeller, Steve Endean, Kerry Woodward, Jean O'Leary, Midge Costanza, Reverend Troy Perry, Barney Frank, Allan Spear, David Goodstein, Sheldon Andelson, David Mixner, and countless others. For the first time, the gay and lesbian rights movement attracted nationally-known or soon-to-be-known politicians: Senator Edward Kennedy, President Jimmy Carter, President Ronald Reagan, Governor Jerry Brown, Senator Diane Feinstein, and Washington, DC, Mayor Marion Barry among others.

The movement engendered a powerful countermovement. Spearheaded by Anita Bryant's 'Save Our Children' Campaign to repeal Dade County, Florida's gay rights ordinance, the message of traditional family values, carried forth by Jerry Falwell and Pat Robertson, led to a rash of anti-gay initiatives and/or the repeal of recently-won expanded civil rights protections inclusive of sexual orientation throughout the late 1970s. Yet, as the movement took shape in the 1970s, it suffered also from repeated internal fractures as lesbians fought to distinguish and ultimately separate from a gay male culture seemingly preoccupied with sodomy reform and other laws related to sexual activity. It struggled through each internal rupture managing to establish numerous lobby organizations and political action committees including the Gay Liberation Front, the Gay Activist Alliance, the National Gay Task Force, the Municipal Elections Committee of Los Angeles, and the Gay Rights National Lobby. The decade ended with the unprecedented March on Washington for Lesbian and Gay Rights on 14 October 1979 that attracted anywhere from the Parks Service estimate of 25,000 to marchers' estimate of 250,000 participants.

By the end of the decade the political side of the gay and lesbian rights movement almost seemed to fizzle faster than any of its predecessors. Spun out of similar concerns that grounded the civil rights and feminist movements, the gay and lesbian rights movement emerged as much of the leftist energy began to wane and as the national culture turned conservative. Having established a vibrant culture and exuberant lifestyle in safe enclaves of San Francisco's Castro or New York City's Greenwich Village, the movement appeared to de-politicize just as it acquired the numbers, public visibility, and cultural confidence to become political. . . .

## Stonewall

Gay liberation, in part, evolved from one transcendental moment which symbolized the shift from victim to empowered agent and came in the late evening of Friday, June 27, 1969 at a seedy gay bar, the Stonewall Inn, in Greenwich Village. Patrons of this particular bar ranged in age from late teens to early thirties and included what historian Toby Marotta has called 'particularly unconventional homosexuals,' e.g., street hustlers and drag queens. When officers raided the bar, numerous customers did not flee the scene. As the police arrested some drag queens, the crowd became restless, and, as escapes were attempted, rioting broke out. The July 3, 1969 edition of *The Village Voice* reported that:

> Limp wrists were forgotten. Beer cans and bottles were heaved at the windows and a rain of coins descended on the cops. . . . Almost by signal the crowd erupted into cobblestone and bottle heaving. . . . From nowhere came an uprooted parking meter— used as a battering ram on the Stonewall door. I heard several cries of 'let's get some gas,' but the blaze of flame which soon appeared in the window of the Stonewall was still a shock.

Perhaps their unconventionality freed these rioters from more reserved tactics; they could rebel because their personal circumstances enabled them to proclaim their homosexuality without the threat of gravely negative circumstances. Before the end of the evening, approximately two thousand individuals battled nearly four hundred police officers.

On Saturday morning a message was haphazardly scrawled on one of the bar's boarded-up windows: 'THEY INVADED OUR RIGHTS . . . LEGALIZE GAY BARS, SUPPORT GAY POWERS.' Rioting continued Saturday evening; by most accounts, it was less violent than the previous evening. On Sunday morning a new sign was posted on the outside of the bar: 'WE HOMOSEXUALS PLEAD WITH OUR PEOPLE TO PLEASE HELP MAINTAIN PEACEFUL AND QUIET CONDUCT ON THE STREETS OF THE VILLAGE—MATTACHINE.' These two messages encapsulate the growing rift of ideology in the existing homophile movement. The former advocated a militant, adversarial, and radical position while the latter maintained more staid and conformist tactics. The use of words such as 'gay' as opposed to 'homosexual' indicate a radical shift in self-perception. Phrases such as 'gay power' belie how dependent the gay liberation movement was on the precedent-setting cultural frames used by both the black power and radical feminist movements. . . .

## The Gay Liberation Front

Liberation theory was organizationally embodied in the Gay Liberation Front (GLF). Gay men and women, but especially the former, disgusted with the moderate tactics and assimilationist aims of the New York Mattachine Society, established this new organization in July of 1969 as a militant arm of the New Left. The GLF proclaimed itself to be 'a revolutionary homosexual group of men and women formed with the realization that complete sexual liberation for all people cannot come about unless existing social institutions are abolished.' The GLF was not preoccupied with discriminatory employment practices, ending police harassment, or repealing of antisodomy laws. The GLF made no explicit statement on the attempt to achieve civil rights legislation or work through the existing political system at all. Rather, as its name suggests, the organization sought liberation from constraint inherent in capitalism itself. It intended to work in concert with all oppressed minorities: women, blacks, workers, and the third world for revolutionary social change.

In order to end structural oppression, the GLF, following the lead of radical feminists, sponsored consciousness-rasing sessions. Consciousness-raising served to bring gay men and women together, to share their experiences, and to discover commonality. Similarity of experience fostered a collective identity. It also encouraged the notion that such similarity could not exist if oppression were not inherent in the system itself. The liberationist ideology that infused consciousness-raising sessions inspired cognitive liberation; it provided gay men and women with a basis to reject legal, medical, and religious definitions of homosexuality and, for the first time, to define themselves. Such definition is apparent in the name 'Gay Liberation Front.' The term homosexual was imposed upon gay men and women by the medical establishment as a term of illness. The term 'homophile' symbolized the assimilationist tactics of the Mattachine and DOB. Radicals chose the word 'gay' because it was how homosexuals referred to each other; the word symbolized self-definition and, as such, was a recognition of internal power.

Gay liberation also fundamentally restructured the definition of 'coming out' in order to build and strengthen a mass movement. Whereas the phrase had previously referred to an individual acknowledgment of homosexuality to oneself, gay liberationists transformed it into an extremely public and political act. Coming out symbolized a total rejection of the negative definitions that society inflicted on the homosexual and substituted both acceptance and pride in one's gayness. Coming out was the ultimate means to conflate the personal and political. Coming out was no longer perceived as a simple one-time act, but as the adoption of an affirmative identity. Furthermore, by acknowledging one's homosexuality, a person exposed himself or herself to social injustice ranging from verbal discrimination to physical violence. Hence, individuals who did come out had a personal tie to the success of a gay liberation movement. Through the process of coming out, the victim status was discarded; homosexuality was transformed from a stigma to be hidden to a source of pride to be celebrated. Indeed, by coming out, the homosexual became gay. Coming out was the necessary psychological break necessary to do what the homophile movement could never accomplish—attract a large following. . . .

The 1970s ushered in an entirely new stage of gay and lesbian rights.

Whereas the GLF had collapsed by 1973, the cognitive liberation produced by a redefinition of 'coming out' and homosexuality itself profoundly affected gays throughout the nation. While the revolution for which liberationist theorists hoped never occurred, the movement witnessed incredible growth. In 1969, before the Stonewall riot, fifty homophile organizations existed in the United States; by 1973, there were over eight hundred gay and lesbian groups, and by the end of the decade they numbered into the thousands. One such organization, the National Gay Task Force established in 1973 and renamed the National Gay and Lesbian Task Force in 1986, would become one of the leading LGBT rights organizations in the United States. Gay bars continued to proliferate, but now gay-friendly and gay-owned health clinics, book stores, cafés, law offices, travel agencies, and churches and synagogues (most notably Troy Perry's [Los Angeles] Metropolitan Community Church) also sprang up. In 1974, the American Psychiatric Association de-listed homosexuality from its register of mental illnesses. In 1975, the ban on gays in the Civil Service was lifted. The gay press expanded, producing magazines and newspapers such as *The Advocate, Washington Blade, Gay Community News, Philadelphia Gay News*, and the *Windy City Times*. Before the end of the decade, Detroit, Boston, Los Angeles, San Franciso, Houston, and Washington, DC, incorporated sexual preference into their civil rights codes. Openly gay and lesbian officials were elected to office including Elaine Noble to the Massachusetts State Assembly, Karen Clark and Allen Spear to the Minnesota State Assembly, and Harvey Milk to the San Francisco Board of Supervisors. In 1980, the Democratic Party adopted a gay and lesbian rights plank at the national convention and an African-American gay man, Mel Boozer, was nominated to be the Democratic Vice Presidential candidate. Before the end of the decade, a national gay and lesbian civil rights bill had been introduced in both the House and Senate. As historian Dennis Altman notes, the 1970s produced a gay male that was 'non-apologetic about his sexuality, self-assertive, highly consumerist and not at all revolutionary, though prepared to demonstrate for gay rights.' Perhaps the most stunning example of the effect that cognitive liberation had on the growth of the movement is that the July 4, 1969 march at Independence Hall in Philadelphia attracted seventy-five participants, whereas the first National March for Lesbian and Gay Rights on 14 October 1979—a mere decade later—attracted between 100,000 and 200,000 participants.

Despite these strides, by the end of the decade a new political conservatism swept across the nation and the gay and lesbian movement encountered an active New Right counter-movement. Anita Bryant spearheaded 'Save Our Children' and rallied for the repeal of a gay rights ordinance in Dade County, Florida, in 1977. Following Bryant's precedent, recently passed gay rights ordinances were repealed in Wichita, Kansas, Eugene, Oregon, and St. Paul, Minnesota. These defeats fostered a massive initiative to prevent passage of the Proposition 6 (the Briggs Initiative) in California. This bill, which advocated the removal of homosexual teachers from public schools, was defeated 58 to 42 per cent after then-Governor Ronald Reagan came out against it. San Francisco Supervisor Harvey Milk was assassinated on 11 November, 1978 by Dan White, an ex-Supervisor; White was convicted of manslaughter and received a sentence of eight years and seven months. Shock at the lenient sentencing on 21 May 1979 led to riots at San Francisco's City Hall. . . .

## 1980s: The Double-Edged Impact of AIDS

In 1981, *The New York Times* reported that five gay men had acquired a curious cancer; in the . . . years since its discovery [from 1981 to 1999], over 300,000 Americans have died from that disease now identified as Acquired Immune Deficiency Syndrome (AIDS), approximately 210,000 of whom were gay men. If only measured in terms of its massively destructive impact, AIDS has fundamentally altered the gay and lesbian movement. Yet, to measure the disease's influence only by positioning the death rate within a specific community dramatically and dangerously oversimplifies how AIDS has affected the movement. In numerous ways, the AIDS crisis produced a variety of positive externalities; however, not only did AIDS provide further anti-gay fodder for the New Right, it also spawned a related but distinct movement increasingly in competition with the equal rights agenda of the gay and lesbian movement. The AIDS movement had distinct aims from the gay and lesbian movement, but, perhaps more importantly, it achieved those aims through strategies never conceived as possible by gay rights activists in the 1970s. AIDS, therefore, dramatically shifted the tactics of sexual minority movement organizations throughout the 1980s and 1990s.

The most immediate impact of AIDS was the incredible rapidity with which it spread throughout the 1980s. By the end of 1981, 225 cases were reported nationwide. In the spring of 1983, this increased to 1,400; only two years later, AIDS cases rose by over 900 per cent to 15,000. In 1987, this figure increased to 40,000 cases reported. The disease's seemingly unstoppable nature coupled with the government and mainstream media's silence and lack of concern regarding both the virus itself and its most prominent class of victims in the United States, i.e., gay men, forced the gay community to mobilize itself. Hundreds of community-based organizations including Shanti, Coming Home Hospice, Project Open Hand of San Francisco, and, most notably, Gay Men's Health Crisis (GMHC), developed to provide services to individuals coping with the virus. The sexual minorities community also shaped the early response by supporting more open and frank discussions of sexuality in the media and by spearheading campaigns for 'safer sex.'

The onset of the AIDS crisis also fostered a dramatic increase in the amount of people who were willing to come out. The lack of an adequate response from the [President Ronald] Reagan and [President George H.W.] Bush administrations forced gay men and women to believe that they were being abandoned by their government. Gay men who would not publicly express their homosexuality in the pre-AIDS era were becoming involved. GMHC itself was started by men who were relatively uninvolved in gay and lesbian politics during the 1970s including Larry Kramer, Nathan Fair, Paul Popham, Paul Rapoport, Larry Mass, and Edmund White. Many of these individuals brought money, contacts, and business experience that pre-AIDS organizations never mustered. . . .

## AIDS Hurt the Movement

However, just as AIDS enabled many of these positive externalities—media visibility, further political organization at the local and national levels, expanded support from both the gay and straight communities, a resurgence of direct action—many of these same benefits carried with them negative impacts on the movement. To mention nothing of the death toll or the vehement attack orchestrated by the New Right, AIDS engendered negative visibility for the gay, lesbian, and bisexual community, fundamentally derailed the movement's original agenda from equal rights to medical and social service provision, and produced an offshoot movement utilizing different methods and having distinct goals.

The New Right exploited AIDS as a weapon with which to maintain inequality, to overturn the achievements of the 1970s, and to return the nation to an era of more traditional heteronormative values. After fighting and winning the de-listing of homosexuality as a mental illness, gays and lesbians now confronted conservatives' use of AIDS to re-link homosexuality with sickness. Two-time Republican candidate for President, Pat Buchanan, furthered the myth that AIDS was a gay disease: 'The poor homosexuals—they have declared war upon nature, and now nature is exacting an awful retribution.' Conservatives discussed quarantining early-identified high risk groups, i.e., gay men, IV drug users, and black and Hispanic men. The United States military imposed mandatory testing. Congress required all immigrants to be tested and forbade entry to anyone who was HIV-positive. Bathhouses and bars, staples of the gay subculture, shut down in record numbers. The ultimate legislative achievement of the New Right was the passage of the Helms Amendment in 1987 which prohibited the use of federal funds to 'provide Aids education, information, or prevention materials and activities that promote or encourage, directly or indirectly, homosexual sexual activities.'

Far more damaging than any attack from conservatives was the derailing effect AIDS had on the celebratory concepts of coming out and gayness introduced by gay liberation philosophy. The visibility that

AIDS conferred on gay men and women was characterized by prominent queer theorist Leo Bersani as 'the visibility of imminent death, of
promised invisibility. Straight America can rest its gaze on us, let us do
our thing over and over in the media, because what our attentive fellow
citizens see is the pathos and impotence of a doomed species.' In this
analysis, homophobic reactions in the media are declining because
AIDS has essentially usurped the role of the homophobe.

## Changes in Activist Strategist

In an effort to attain media coverage and government support in
combating the virus, many gay and lesbian organizations attempted
to 'de-gay' AIDS and de-sexualize homosexuality. Existing institutionalized homophobia meant that AIDS could not be successfully com-
bated if it was continually thought of as a 'gay disease.' In promoting
the truthful notion that heterosexuals were also susceptible, the gay
and lesbian movement abandoned the overarching and long-term
aims of equality and fighting institutionalized homophobia for the
immediate need of survival. 'De-gaying' the disease also inhibited
people from coming out since people could donate to AIDS organizations without the stigma of being associated with a gay organization.
'De-gaying' has also paradoxically led to a measure of invisibility of a
minority which accounts for 70 per cent of all AIDS cases in the
United States. For example, at the 1987 March on Washington, no
mention was given to the gay or lesbian community in the program
regarding the Names Project AIDS Quilt nor during the five speeches
given during the candlelight vigil.

While AIDS did attract wider participation from the gay and
straight communities, especially among upper middle-class gay men,
such participation further steered the movement away from its traditionally leftist orientation. The influx of this group, while bringing
immense resources, also brought political conservatism: 'in place of
liberation, the AIDS movement substituted nondiscrimination; instead of building a movement, it built agencies and bureaucracies;
instead of placing its political faith in training and organizing gay and
lesbian people, and our allies, into an electoral coalition, it placed
faith in friends in high places.' This more conservative tendency also
led to a de-sexualization of homosexuality itself, disregarding the con-
nection between sexual freedom and gay liberation; since AIDS
exposed gay sexuality, gay men and women often responded by de-
emphasizing that liberated sexuality and promoting a new image es-
pousing monogamy and safer sex. . . .

## The Gay 90s and Beyond: (In)visibility and the Movement Today

The American gay and lesbian movement, or rather gayness in general, has become increasingly visible in politics and popular culture

throughout the 1990s. Enormous volumes of pro- and anti-gay legislation have been debated, passed, and rejected mostly at the state level, but also at the national level, and the movement has continued to fight against an increasingly powerful Christian right. Yet, such visibility, while enormously powerful in promoting the civil rights–based agenda of the movement, has revealed the multiple factions that currently exist in the movement—most importantly, the exclusion of people of color—as well as threatened the viability of earlier liberationist aims to end institutionalized heterosexism. While gays and lesbians may have received new prominence in national electoral politics—revealed by the 1992 presidential election and the resurgence of controversy over 'Don't Ask, Don't Tell'[1] and hate crimes legislation in the 2000 election—the movement also demonstrated its political weakness and lagging mainstream cultural acceptance at the national level by its inability to achieve a full lifting of the ban on homosexuals in the military, its failure to secure passage of the Employment Non-Discrimination Act (ENDA) in 1996, and its inability to secure national hate crimes legislation.

Throughout the 1970s and the 1980s, the struggle for gay rights has been viewed as a primarily white male movement. The concerns of women and people of color were never foremost on the gay agenda. The essential 'whiteness' of the movement became startlingly visible as gay African-Americans, Asians, and Latinos established separate sexual minority rights and AIDS organizations to help members of those particular ethnic minorities cope with both civil rights violations and the illness. The establishment of the Latino/a Lesbian and Gay Organization (LLEGO), the Native American AIDS Task Force, the National Gay Asian and Pacific Islander Network, and the National Black Gay and Lesbian Leadership Forum revealed that mainstream gay and AIDS organizations failed to recognize internalized elements of racism and sexism. . . .

## Into the Mainstream

The 1992 election found the incumbent Republican President Bush battling an economic recession, a gay minority and its straight supporters increasingly disillusioned with the Republican response to AIDS, and an increasingly powerful Christian right which aimed to revive 'traditional' family values. AIDS and the Right's negative response towards the disease brought gay issues to the forefront of the election forcing each Democratic contender to take a stance on gay rights. The position they took contrasted starkly to their Republican opponents. Every major Democratic candidate promised to increase AIDS funding and to lift the ban on gays in the military. Gay rights had been a topic on which the Democratic Party had wavered since

1. the military policy against asking personnel if they are homosexual

the 1972 election, and which party leadership had chosen to down-
play in 1988 after Walter Mondale's poor showing against Ronald Reagan in 1984. However, the gay constituency had money and votes.
Indeed, Bill Clinton's emergence as the candidate to receive the overall endorsement of the gay community had less to do with his stance
on gay rights—a law criminalizing same-sex sodomy was passed while
he was attorney general of Arkansas—and more to do with the fact
that he actively sought the gay vote, in direct contrast to anti-gay
Republican sentiment couched in traditional family values rhetoric.
Nor did the help of an openly gay political consultant, David Mixner,
harm Clinton's campaign. Mixner advised Clinton to tailor his
speeches to stress the inclusion of gays and lesbians in his cabinet as
well as a sincere desire to use federal resources to stem the AIDS crisis.
An estimated 75 per cent of the gay vote helped Clinton secure the
presidency. . . .

The movement has attained a high degree of visibility in the political arena in the 1990s through the 'don't ask, don't tell' compromise;
ironically, the policy was, in part, intended to maintain gay invisibility within the military. No longer is the homosexual act grounds for
discharge, but rather the mere verbal expression of the act. According
to theorist Leo Bersani, coercing soldiers to keep their sexual orientation secret illustrates an awareness of the potential threat of queer
politics to the maintenance of patriarchal institutions. The enforced
silence further bolsters, or at least avoids the destabilization of, het-
eronormativity. . . .

The movement is still far from achieving its most fundamental
aim: the destruction of institutionalized homophobia or even the passage of national level civil rights legislation inclusive of sexual orientation. The maintenance and, indeed, strengthening of the military
ban as well as the power and popular resonance of Christian right
anti-gay rhetoric, vividly reflect this failure. In order to counter successfully the mobilization of the far right, the movement must create
a dual agenda focusing on civil rights legislation at all government
levels, on the one hand, and liberation and cultural reform on the
other. It must combine a grassroots with a top-down approach to
ensure that its constituents are mobilized and their voices heard.

# Gay and Lesbian Artists During the Harlem Renaissance

Alden Reimonenq

African American artists led the cultural development that came to be known as the Harlem Renaissance during the 1920s and 1930s. Recently readers have renewed their interest in the literary works produced during this era. Contemporary black feminist scholars have underscored the importance of sexuality in the creative lives of Harlem Renaissance women, including bisexual or lesbian writers and performers such as Angelina Weld Grimké, Alice Dunbar-Nelson, Bessie Smith, and Ma Rainey. In this selection Alden Reimonenq contends that scholars should also examine the role of homosexuality in the development of the Harlem Renaissance since the major male figures of the period were bisexual or gay artists, including Langston Hughes, Alain Locke, and Countee Cullen. Reimonenq examines the thriving black gay culture during the Harlem Renaissance and surveys the contributions of major gay, lesbian, and bisexual artists. Reimonenq serves as the dean of the College of Arts, Letters, and Social Sciences at the California State University at Hayward. He is the author and editor of many books and articles about African American gays, including *Milking Black Bull: 11 Gay Black Poets*. He is currently writing a biography of Harlem Renaissance poet Countee Cullen.

The Harlem Renaissance, an African-American literary movement of the 1920s and 1930s, included several important gay and lesbian writers.

In African-American literary history, the 1920s and 1930s have been variously labeled the Jazz Age, the era of the New Negro, and most commonly the Harlem Renaissance. Scholars debate the beginning and ending of the period; others question whether a "renaissance" occurred at all.

Although most commentators agree that this period saw an unpar-

alleled outpouring of artistic achievement and claim that this "movement" was successful in creating foundational steps in the long
African-American arts tradition, still others hold that the renaissance
was a failure.

## Reviving the Past

In recent years, the reading public has welcomed the recuperated literary reputations of many Harlem Renaissance figures as their works
have been republished, researched, and studied.

The Black Feminist movement has been a major force in validating
and cementing canonical spaces for Jessie Fauset, Nella Larsen, Zora
Neale Hurston, Angelina Grimké, Alice Dunbar-Nelson, Georgia Douglas Johnson, and others. Black feminist scholars have also been forth-
right in foregrounding the sexualities of these women as a prominent
feature of their creative energies.

For example, Gloria T. Hull has written honestly and intelligently of
black lesbianism as critical to understanding the works of Grimké and
Dunbar-Nelson. Studies of the male artists of the period, however,
have, so far, only flirted with issues of sexuality in general and have
ignored, denied, or dismissed homosexuality as an artistic influence.

It is indeed surprising that discussions of the Harlem Renaissance
have not involved in-depth investigations of homosexuality when, in
fact, the major male figures of the period were gay or bisexual: Alain
Locke, Countee Cullen, Langston Hughes, Claude McKay, Wallace
Thurman, Richard Bruce Nugent, and even the famous white sponsor
Cart Van Vechten.

With the burgeoning interest in gay studies, however, scholars are
beginning to research the lives and works of these artists in order to
evaluate the ways in which homosexuality functioned as a liberating
and constricting force.

## Homosexuality and the Writers of the Harlem Renaissance

[Scholar] Eric Garber's study creates a picturesque montage of Harlem
gay life during this period when many African Americans tolerated,
indulged in, and even celebrated homosexuality. Garber's is a cine-
matic look at gay life, art, and culture that pauses here and there to
capture the details of the night club scene, art work, personalities, and
so on.

Painting Harlem as a gay liberated capital, Garber shows how
homosexuality, among intellectuals especially, was accepted as a personal matter that did not interfere with the larger, more important
work in racial and cultural advancement. Gays were oppressed during
the period, but a thriving black gay subculture ensured that open
secrets were kept.

Bessie Smith, Ma Rainey, "Moms" Mabley, Mabel Hampton, Alberta

Hunter, Gladys Bentley, and other lesbian or bisexual women found employment in show business, and many sang the blues about gay lives and loves.

Drag balls, commonplace during the period, were called "spectacles of color" by Langston Hughes in *The Big Sea* (1945); such balls were frequented often by the Harlem bohemians who wrote candidly about them in their correspondence.

Speakeasies and buffet flats (rental units notorious for cafeteria-style opportunities for a variety of sex) were spaces in which gays were granted generous liberation. Wallace Thurman, in *Infants of the Spring* (1932), gives a realistic rendering of the buffet flat that he, Langston Hughes, and Richard Bruce Nugent shared from time to time.

This artistic community was a complex one with an intricate network of members that cut across all sectors of the art world. At a time when New York still had laws banning homosexuality and when baths and gay bars were raided frequently, it is noteworthy that the Harlem Renaissance was moved along, in great measure, by gay men and women who led amazing double lives.

## The Function of the Closet

The function of the closet [keeping homosexuality a secret] during this period is complex. Although the closet has typically been seen as oppressive, many of these gay artists subverted the stultifying power of the closet by forming an artistic coalition grounded in secrecy and loyalty. Thus, the closet was reconstructed to form a protective shield against discrimination from publishers, patrons, and the media. The closet enabled many writers to blend into the mainstream and to publish without the fear of exposure.

## The Influence of Alain Locke

Alain Locke (1886–1954), who has been credited with ushering in the New Negro movement, has been justly criticized for advancing the careers of young black males to the obvious neglect of such writers as Grimké, Dunbar-Nelson, and Georgia Douglas Johnson. Locke, a Harvard Ph.D. and professor at Howard University, promoted the careers of Wallace Thurman, Richard Bruce Nugent, Countee Cullen, and Langston Hughes.

To crown only Locke with the accolade of inspiring the Harlem Renaissance is to deny the seminal positions held by W.E.B. DuBois, Jessie Fauset, James Weldon Johnson, and the *Opportunity* and *Crisis* [journal] organizations in fostering the careers of many of the period's artists.

Without question a misogynist, Locke's contribution to the development of a gay male literary heritage was formidable and certainly deliberate. He was at the center of the Harlem gay coterie and very early on gave impetus to the careers of Cullen and, especially, Hughes.

## Countee Cullen

Through frequent letters, Locke urged Countee Cullen (1903–1946) to write poetry aimed at bettering the race. Urging Cullen to read Edward Carpenter's anthology of male-male friendship *Ioläus*, Locke helped the young writer find comfort in realizing his gay self. Thus, Locke was also, in part, responsible for Cullen's maturing gay sensibilities.

Cullen learned the importance of the closet and wrote poetry that promoted the image and idea of the New Negro while also subtly expressing his gay self. Scholars are beginning to investigate the coded language in Cullen's poetry in order to establish him as a leading figure in the black gay male literary heritage. Many of the lyrics in *The Black Christ and Other Poems* (1929) and *The Medea and Some Poems* (1935) lend themselves to gay readings.

Yet, in as early a work as *Color* (1925), Cullen wrote gay verses, such as "Tableau," "Fruit of the Flower," and "For a Poet"—a poem written at a time when Cullen was embroiled in unrequited love for Langston Hughes.

## Langston Hughes

Before he had finished college at Lincoln University in Pennsylvania and during his many travels, Langston Hughes (1902–1967) was pursued by Locke, with Cullen mediating. Although sexual relationships never materialized, the intimate friendships of these three gay men were concretized in their commitment to their literary careers and shared racial ideologies.

Although there were regular philosophical disagreements regarding the bewildering vocation of poets who were also deemed "race men," still a tight bond developed that knit these writers together for their entire lives.

Hughes, arguably the most closeted of the renaissance gay males, had many close associations with homosexuals and lesbians throughout his life. And, as with Cullen, scholars are beginning to decipher the codification of his gayness in his poetry, drama, and fiction.

Commentators have cited many poems as candidates for gay readings, among them "Young Sailor," "Waterfront Streets," "Desire," "Trumpet Player," "Café 3 A.M.," and the sequence of poems in *Montage of a Dream Deferred* (1951).

## Angelina Weld Grimké

Angelina Weld Grimké (1880–1958) made her contribution to the lesbian literary heritage as a poet during the Harlem Renaissance. She was published in Locke's *The New Negro* (1925) and in Cullen's *Caroling Dusk* (1927). Grimké's love lyrics, many as yet unpublished, are mostly addressed to women and describe love that is hidden, unrequited, or otherwise unrealized.

The honesty of the lesbian passion in these beautiful lyrics secures for Grimké a place in African-American gay literature. Poems such as "Rosalie," "If," "To Her of the Cruel Lips," "El Beso," "Autumn," "Give Me Your Eyes," "Caprichosa," and "My Shrine" are all testimony to the unrealized lesbian love for which Grimké longed.

## Alice Dunbar-Nelson

Alice Dunbar-Nelson (1875–1935) was married several times, most notably to the poet Paul Laurence Dunbar. All of her marriages were troublesome for one reason or another, but despite her personal problems, she managed to write and publish fiction and poetry. The lesbian relationships that checkered her life had a significant influence on her creativity. For example, Gloria T. Hull suggests that, in the unpublished novel *This Lofty Oak*, Dunbar-Nelson chronicles the life of Edwina B. Kruse, one of her lovers.

Dunbar-Nelson's literary reputation during the Harlem Renaissance is assessed largely (and Hull contends erroneously) on her achievement as a poet. She published "Violets" in *Crisis* in 1917, a work that exemplifies the polish and lucidity that typify her poetry, especially her sonnets.

Hull documents other lesbian affairs with Fay Jackson Robinson, a Los Angeles journalist, and Helene Ricks London, a Bermuda artist. Dunbar-Nelson wrote poetry for these women, most of which does not survive except in diary fragments. Dunbar-Nelson's diary reveals her prominent place in an active network of African-American lesbians.

## Claude McKay

In *Home to Harlem* (1927), Jamaican-born Claude McKay (1899–1948) openly discusses Harlem's black experience with lesbianism and even has a significant black gay male character. Following Wayne F. Coopers fine biography of McKay (which discusses honestly the writer's homosexuality), scholars are beginning to make connections between the writer's sexuality and his writing.

Yet, as is the case with many of the renaissance writers, McKay's homosexuality as an influence on his creativity must be traced by reading between the lines. Some poems seem to be perfect candidates for such readings, among them "Bennie's Departure," "To Inspector W. E. Clark," "Alfonso, Dressing to Wait at Table," "The Barrier," "Courage," "Adolescence," "Home Thoughts," and "On Broadway."

Other poems, such as "Desolate" and "Absence," can easily be given gay readings, inasmuch as gays often write on the themes of isolation, dreams deferred, unrequited or secret love, and alienation.

## Wallace Thurman

The short life of Wallace Thurman (1902–1934) gave to the African-American gay and lesbian tradition two novels—*The Blacker the Berry*

(1929) and *Infants of the Spring* (1932)—which are unmatched as clear and honest depictions of black gay and lesbian life.

## Richard Bruce Nugent

The long life of Richard Bruce Nugent (1906–1989) produced very few literary monuments, but like Thurman, Nugent had a penchant for shocking readers and producing works with a decidedly foreign and provocative voice. Locke included Nugent's gay story "Sahdji" in *The New Negro* and encouraged the young writer to work at narrative.

In 1926, the one and only issue of *Fire!!* (a quarterly "Devoted to the Younger Negro Artists"), carried Nugent's more developed homosexual story "Smoke, Lilies, and Jade"—now praised as the first published African-American gay short story. The story is the fictionalization of an evening Nugent spent walking and talking with Langston Hughes.

The story is a major achievement in gay literary history because it can be read as a defense of homosexuality while it also poignantly thematizes male-male love as beautifully natural and wholesome.

Even in his later years, Nugent continued to write openly about the gay experience: In 1970, *Crisis* published a Christmas story, "Beyond Where the Star Stood Still," in which Herod's catamite offers a remarkable gift to the infant Jesus. Again, Nugent—embracing the mushrooming Gay Rights movement—aimed at forcing the safe African-American world, shaped largely by the fundamentalist church, to face the reality of a black gay presence.

## Subverting the Mainstream Power Establishments

Although Harlem was awash with gay literary production during the renaissance, it would be overstating reality to say that there was a deliberate gay movement afoot. Homosexuality might have found toleration in the privacy of speakeasies and salon parties, but the boardrooms at major publishing companies were far less inviting.

Couple that fact with the conservatism that underlined the very notion of a "Talented Tenth,"[1] and it is easy to conclude that any gay literary production (with the clear exception of Thurman and Nugent, who were severely criticized) would have to subvert, in rather creative ways, the mainstream white and black power establishments.

## Recurring Themes, Issues, and Ideas

The recurring themes, issues, and ideas in the gay and lesbian writing of the period underscore the endurance of those writers who strove to express their gay selves.

A recurrent motif in the writings of the period is the presence of a

1. Many Harlem Renaissance leaders believed that the "Talented Tenth," or the intellectual elite, would bring the rest of the African-American race into greater equality with other Americans.

forbidden, unnamed, and genderless love. Also common is the use of nature to express the budding forth of an unquestionable though unutterable beauty that is often unappreciated and wasted. Most writers stutter through expressions of a kind of passion so noble yet so unattainable that it must be enacted secretively or abandoned.

Because sexuality is inextricably wound up in the very experience of being human, it often shares turf with deep religious experience or political conviction. Cullen's "The Black Christ," for example, is on the surface a narrative poem of salvation. Yet the poet weaves the salvation experience neatly into the somewhat veiled story of Jim's questionable sexuality.

The homoeroticism of the poem pictures the lynched black boy as a beauty of nature who is raped and sacrificed because he goes unappreciated. Ironically, he is falsely accused and killed for attempting to rape a beautiful white girl whom he understands as the embodiment of Spring. The poem, like many of the period, can be read on a deeper, less apparent level as a diatribe against sexual repression.

Perhaps the most prevalent theme among gay writers of the period is that of the unrealized or displaced dream. One cannot read Grimké, Hughes, McKay, or Cullen without confronting the unachievable, unnamed, and haunting dream.

From the most closeted to the most liberated, the writers of the gay Harlem Renaissance form an unquestionable tradition through which contemporary gay and lesbian readers can see the depth and range of experiences that, in many cases, mirror theirs. If these mirrored images have the power to transform and liberate, perhaps the new renaissance currently underway by African-American gay and lesbian writers will produce a literature that represents more realized and fulfilling dreams.

# GAY AND LESBIAN PERSECUTION IN NAZI GERMANY

United States Holocaust Memorial Museum

During the Holocaust homosexuals, Jews, and other minorities were persecuted by the Nazis. The Third Reich viewed gays as weak and unable to fight for the German nation. In addition, gays seemed unlikely to reproduce and contribute to the Nazi goal of strengthening the Aryan race. Third Reich commandants created the Reich Special Office for the Combating of Homosexuality and Abortion to harass and imprison gays and women seeking abortions. This excerpt from the United States Holocaust Memorial Museum Web site documents the many ways in which the Nazis persecuted gays and lesbians, including destroying anything related to gay culture and research about homosexuality, shutting down gay bars and organizations, and sending gays to death camps. Lesbians were also persecuted by the Nazis, though not to the extent that gays were. The United States Holocaust Memorial Museum is America's national institution for the documentation, study, and interpretation of Holocaust history.

On September 1, 1935, this harsher, amended version of Paragraph 175 of the [German] Criminal Code, originally framed in 1871, went into effect. Under this revised law and the creation of the Reich Special Office for the Combating of Homosexuality and Abortion: Special office (II S), the number of prosecutions increased sharply, peaking in the years 1937–1939. Half of all convictions for homosexual activity under the Nazi regime occurred during these years.

> 175. A male who commits lewd and lascivious acts with another male or permits himself to be so abused for lewd and lascivious acts, shall be punished by imprisonment. In a case of a participant under 21 years of age at the time of the commission of the act, the court may, in especially slight cases, refrain from punishment.

United States Holocaust Memorial Museum, "Persecution of Homosexuals in the Third Reich," and "Lesbians and the Third Reich," www.ushmm.org, 2002.

175a. Confinement in a penitentiary not to exceed ten years and, under extenuating circumstances, imprisonment for not less than three months shall be imposed:

1. Upon a male who, with force or with threat of imminent danger to life and limb, compels another male to commit lewd and lascivious acts with him or compels the other party to submit to abuse for lewd and lascivious acts;

2. Upon a male who, by abuse of a relationship of dependence upon him, in consequence of service, employment, or subordination, induces another male to commit lewd and lascivious acts with him or to submit to being abused for such acts;

3. Upon a male who being over 21 years of age induces another male under 21 years of age to commit lewd and lascivious acts with him or to submit to abuse for lewd and lascivious acts;

4. Upon a male who professionally engages in lewd and lascivious acts with other men, or submits to such abuse by other men, or offers himself for lewd and lascivious acts with other men.

175b. Lewd and lascivious acts contrary to nature between human beings and animals shall be punished by imprisonment; loss of civil rights may also be imposed.

## Persecution of Homosexuals in the Third Reich

While male homosexuality remained illegal in Weimar Germany [1919–1933] under Paragraph 175 of the criminal code, German homosexual-rights activists became worldwide leaders in efforts to reform societal attitudes that condemned homosexuality. Many in Germany regarded the Weimar Republic's toleration of homosexuals as a sign of Germany's decadence. The Nazis posed as moral crusaders who wanted to stamp out the "vice" of homosexuality from Germany in order to help win the racial struggle. Once they took power in 1933, the Nazis intensified persecution of German male homosexuals. Persecution ranged from the dissolution of homosexual organizations to internment in concentration camps.

The Nazis believed that male homosexuals were weak, effeminate men who could not fight for the German nation. They saw homosexuals as unlikely to produce children and increase the German birthrate. The Nazis held that inferior races produced more children than "Aryans," so anything that diminished Germany's reproductive potential was considered a racial danger.

SS [paramilitary *schutzstaffel*] chief Heinrich Himmler directed the increasing persecution of homosexuals in the Third Reich. Lesbians were not regarded as a threat to Nazi racial policies and were generally not targeted for persecution. Similarly, the Nazis generally did not target non-German homosexuals unless they were active with German partners. In most cases, the Nazis were prepared to accept former homosexuals into the "racial community" provided that they became "racially conscious" and gave up their lifestyle.

## Escalating Intolerance

On May 6, 1933, students led by Storm Troopers (Sturmabteilung; SA) broke into the Institute for Sexual Science in Berlin and confiscated its unique library. Four days later, most of this collection of over 12,000 books and 35,000 irreplaceable pictures was destroyed along with thousands of other "degenerate" works of literature in the book burning in Berlin's city center. The remaining materials were never recovered. Magnus Hirschfeld, the founder of the Institute and a pioneer in the scientific study of human sexuality, was lecturing in France at the time and chose not to return to Germany.

The destruction of the Institute was a first step toward eradicating an openly gay or lesbian culture from Germany. Police closed bars and clubs such as the "Eldorado" and banned publications such as *Die Freundschaft* (Friendship). In this early stage the Nazis drove homosexuals underground, destroying their networks of support. In 1934, the Gestapo (secret state police) instructed local police forces to keep lists of all men engaged in homosexual activities. Police in many parts of Germany had in fact been doing this for years. The Nazis used these "pink lists" to hunt down individual homosexuals during police actions.

On June 28, 1935, the Ministry of Justice revised Paragraph 175. The revisions provided a legal basis for extending Nazi persecution of homosexuals. Ministry officials expanded the category of "criminally indecent activities between men" to include any act that could be construed as homosexual. The courts later decided that even intent or thought sufficed. On October 26, 1936, Himmler formed within the Security Police the Reich Central Office for Combating Abortion and Homosexuality. Josef Meisinger, executed in 1947 for his brutality in occupied Poland, led the new office. The police had powers to hold in protective custody or preventive arrest those deemed dangerous to Germany's moral fiber, jailing indefinitely—without trial—anyone they chose. In addition, homosexual prisoners just released from jail were immediately re-arrested and sent to concentration camps if the police thought it likely that they would continue to engage in homosexual acts.

From 1937 to 1939, the peak years of the Nazi persecution of homosexuals, the police increasingly raided homosexual meeting places, seized address books, and created networks of informers and undercover agents to identify and arrest suspected homosexuals. On

April 4, 1938, the Gestapo issued a directive indicating that men convicted of homosexuality could be incarcerated in concentration
camps. Between 1933 and 1945 the police arrested an estimated
100,000 men as homosexuals. Most of the 50,000 men sentenced by
the courts spent time in regular prisons, and between 5,000 and
15,000 were interned in concentration camps.

## Homosexual Internment

The Nazis interned some homosexuals in concentration camps immediately after the seizure of power in January 1933. Those interned
came from all areas of German society, and often had only the cause
of their imprisonment in common. Some homosexuals were interned
under other categories by mistake, and the Nazis purposefully miscat-
egorized some political prisoners as homosexuals. Prisoners marked
by pink triangles to signify homosexuality were treated harshly in the
camps. According to many survivor accounts, homosexuals were
among the most abused groups in the camps.

Because some Nazis believed homosexuality was a sickness that
could be cured, they designed policies to "cure" homosexuals of their
"disease" through humiliation and hard work. Guards ridiculed and
beat homosexual prisoners upon arrival, often separating them from
other inmates. Rudolf Hoess, commandant of Auschwitz, wrote in his
memoirs that homosexuals were segregated in order to prevent homosexuality from spreading to other inmates and guards. Personnel in
charge of work details in the Dora-Mittelbau underground rocket fac-
tory or in the stone quarries at Flossenbuerg and Buchenwald often
gave deadly assignments to homosexuals.

## Surviving Persecution

Survival in camps took on many forms. Some homosexual inmates
secured administrative and clerical jobs. For other prisoners, sexuality
became a means of survival. In exchange for sexual favors, some
Kapos [inmates chosen to control their peers] protected a chosen prisoner, usually of young age, giving him extra food and shielding him
from the abuses of other prisoners. Homosexuals themselves very
rarely became Kapos due to the lack of a support network. Kapo
guardianship was no protection against the guards' brutality, of
course. In any case, the Kapo often tired of an individual, sometimes
killing him and finding another on the next transport. Though individual homosexual inmates could secure a measure of protection in
some ways, as a group homosexual prisoners lacked the support network common to other groups. Without this help in mitigating brutality, homosexual prisoners were unlikely to survive long.

One avenue of survival available to some homosexuals was castration, which some criminal justice officials advocated as a way of "cur-
ing" sexual deviance. Homosexual defendants in criminal cases or

concentration camps could agree to castration in exchange for lower sentences. Later, judges and SS camp officials could order castration without the consent of a homosexual prisoner.

Nazis interested in finding a "cure" for homosexuality expanded this program to include medical experimentation on homosexual inmates of concentration camps. These experiments caused illness, mutilation, and even death, and yielded no scientific knowledge.

There are no known statistics for the number of homosexuals who died in the camps. . . .

## Lesbians and the Third Reich

Although homosexual acts among men had traditionally been a criminal offense throughout much of Germany, lesbianism (homosexual acts among women) was not criminalized. This was true in large part because of the subordinate role of women in German state and society. Unlike male homosexuals, lesbians were not generally regarded as a social or political threat. Even after the Nazi rise to power in 1933, most lesbians in Germany were able to live relatively quiet lives, generally undisturbed by the police.

Although they were hampered by the inferior roles ascribed to women in Imperial Germany, lesbians had been part of the homosexual emancipation movement in Germany since the 1890s. German law prohibited women from joining political organizations until 1908. Even after the easing of this restriction women were discouraged from political activity, so lesbians turned to more informal gatherings in bars and clubs. This trend coincided with a general easing of sexual morality in Germany after World War I. The Weimar Republic brought with it new social and political freedoms. For most homosexual men and lesbian women in Germany, the Weimar era was a time of relative openness.

Berlin and other major cities became centers of homosexual life in Germany. In Berlin, clubs like the "Dorian Gray" and "The Magic Flute Dance Palace" helped create a lesbian social network, making it easier for urban lesbians to live openly than for those in more rural areas of Germany. The easing of censorship restrictions led to a variety of lesbian literature including the journals *Frauenliebe* (Female Love) and *Die Freundin* (Girlfriend).

## The Beginning of Repression

Traditional political and social conservatives harshly criticized this new openness for homosexuals in Germany. The resurgence of political conservatism in the later years of the Weimar Republic led to a new series of repressive measures against homosexuals. In 1928, for example, the police banned *Die Freundin* and other lesbian literature based on the Protection of Youth from Obscene Publications Act. Many conservatives demanded the enactment of criminal statutes against lesbian sexual acts. Pamphleteers such as Erhard Eberhard wrote tracts against homosexuals, feminists, Republicans, and Jews, groups that were often linked by conservatives to a conspiracy to destroy Germany. In particular they denounced the movement for women's rights, claiming it was really a front for seducing German women into lesbianism.

With the rise of the Nazis to power in 1933, this conservative backlash was replaced with state repression. The Nazis believed women were not only inferior to men but also by nature dependent on them; therefore, they considered lesbians to be less threatening than male homosexuals. The Nazis regarded women as passive, especially in sexual matters, and in need of men to fulfill their lives and participate in sex. Many Nazis also worried that the more explicit social affection between individual women blurred the lines between friendship and lesbianism, making more difficult the task of ferreting out "true" lesbians. Finally, the Nazis dismissed lesbianism as a state and social problem because they believed lesbians could still carry out a German woman's primary role: to be a mother of as many "Aryan" babies as possible. Every woman, regardless of her sexuality, could serve the Nazi state as wife and mother.

## Different Forms of Persecution

The Nazis nonetheless persecuted lesbians, albeit less severely than they persecuted male homosexuals. Soon after Hitler's appointment as chancellor, the police systematically raided and closed down homosexual meeting bars and clubs, forcing lesbians to meet in secret. The Nazis created a climate of fear by encouraging police raids and denunciations against lesbians. Many lesbians broke off contacts with their circles of friends, some moving to new cities where they would be unknown. Others even sought the protection of marriage, entering into marriages of convenience with male homosexual friends.

While the police regarded lesbians as "asocials"—people who did not conform to Nazi norms and therefore could be arrested or sent to concentration camps—few were imprisoned because of their sexuality alone. The Nazis did not classify lesbians as homosexual prisoners, and only male homosexual prisoners had to wear the pink triangle. Though police arrests of lesbians were comparatively rare, the threat of persecution made living openly as a lesbian dangerous.

Lesbians also suffered discrimination because of the Nazis' policy toward German women in general. Since the Nazis believed women should serve primarily as wives and mothers, they forced women out of prestigious careers. Paradoxically, labor demands brought on by rearmament and the war actually increased the number of working women, though they were relegated to work in low-paying jobs. The low wages set for women particularly affected lesbians, since lesbians were generally unmarried and could not rely on a husband's job for support. Economic hardships combined with ever-increasing social pressures and fear of arrest to make the lives of lesbians difficult even though sexual acts between females were not illegal in Nazi Germany.

Though many lesbians experienced hardships during the Third Reich, the Nazis did not systematically persecute them. Those who were willing to be discreet and inconspicuous, marry male friends, or otherwise seem to conform to the expectations of society were often left alone and survived.

# A Symbol of Gay Pride: The Stonewall Riots of 1969

John D'Emilio

On June 27, 1969, a group of gay and lesbian customers at the New York Stonewall Inn resisted a police raid and began a protest against discrimination and harassment that has become well known as the Stonewall riots. The event has achieved mythic status in the gay liberation movement. In the following selection John D'Emilio argues that although the Stonewall rebellion has become a potent symbol of grassroots resistance, most accounts of the event perpetuate false assumptions about the struggle for gay and lesbian rights in the United States. Drawing from his experiences as an activist and his knowledge as a scholar of gay and lesbian history, D'Emilio asserts that the modern gay rights campaign started before Stonewall. Moreover, many struggles for social change were waged in settings other than street demonstrations like the Stonewall rebellion. While many insist that only the most oppressed people can lead struggles for gay rights, D'Emilio contends that gays and lesbians from privileged or affluent backgrounds also contribute to the gay liberation movement. D'Emilio is a professor of history and the director of the Gender and Women's Studies Program at the University of Illinois in Chicago. He is the author and editor of numerous books and articles about gay and lesbian history, including *The World Turned: Essays on Gay History, Politics, and Culture* and *Sexual Politics, Sexual Communities: The Making of a Homosexual Minority in the United States, 1940–1970.*

Growing up Catholic in New York City in the 1950s, I could never escape the palpable presence of St. Patrick. His feast was a holiday in the city's parochial schools, and one of the local television stations dropped its regular programming to broadcast the St. Patrick's Day Parade along Fifth Avenue in Manhattan. The day before, when school was in session, ethnic pride burst forth as Irish American students and teachers sported various items of green clothing. Even the local bakers cooperated in the celebration, with cookies, cupcakes, and pastries of every sort sprouting green frosting.

As an Italian in an Irish parish and neighborhood, I experienced St. Patrick's Day as a hostile assault. My Irish friends suddenly metamorphosed into marauding gangs attacking all the guineas and wops who, perversely they felt, refused to wear green. My parents, aunts, and uncles grumbled at home because their children *had* to march in the school's parade contingent in the bitter late winter cold, while no comparable requirement was enforced for Columbus Day, the closest Italian equivalent. I hated every minute of the annual festivities and came to dread their yearly arrival.

My fifth grade instructor, Miss Schretlen, was the only non-Irish teacher in our school, and she offered me an opportunity to bring the Irish down a notch. As St. Patrick's Day approached, she proposed a class debate on the question, "Did St. Patrick drive the snakes out of Ireland?" When she asked for volunteers, my hand shot up to present and defend the negative side of the proposition.

It was my first research project. For days beforehand, I foreswore after-school play and, instead, ensconced myself in the local public library. I read every encyclopedia I could find. I accumulated reams of evidence demonstrating that St. Patrick could not have accomplished this miraculous deed because, geologically, Ireland never had any snakes to be driven out! When the time for the debate arrived, I listened as my opponent simply repeated the tired old stories about St. Patrick's achievements. Then, I confidently addressed the class, presenting what I knew was an airtight case. When Miss Schretlen cared for a vote, I lost by a two-to-one majority. All the Irish students voted their faith. The rest of the class, an outnumbered minority, voted for me. It was my first lesson in the power of symbol and myth.

## The Stonewall Myth

Stonewall is our symbol of resistance, our myth of emancipation from oppression. As the years separating us from the riot grow, so does its power. In the biggest cities, the whole month of June has become a cornucopia of gay and lesbian delights, with theater productions, film festivals, political forums, museum exhibitions, and other events giving substance to our community's pride and strength and culminating in a massive outpouring on gay freedom day. In smaller cities, the ability to mount a march in honor of Stonewall figures as a metaphorical coming of age. Stonewall's power is so great that it resonates for gay men and lesbians around the world: The riot is commemorated on several continents. . . .

The story of Stonewall has been retold in print too many times to count. Hardly a book about gay and lesbian life fails to make some mention of it, to describe in bareboned fashion what happened and what it was all about. A typical account goes something like this: Late on Friday evening, June 27, 1969, police came to raid the Stonewall Inn, a gay bar on Christopher Street in Greenwich Village. As they led patrons to the waiting vans, a crowd gathered. The patrons of the bar, many of whom were young, nonwhite, effeminate, and given to both camp and drag, began to resist and, with the support of the crowd, a full-scale riot developed. The following night, there was more street fighting in the Village. Thus was born a gay liberation movement.

No one but a fool would dispute the historical significance of the Stonewall riot. Yet, while its importance is not debatable, its meaning is most definitely up for grabs. As with all myths and symbols, we do more than retell and remember it. We *interpret* it. We extract lessons from the event and, in doing so, shape an understanding of the past and the present. Embedded in the story of Stonewall that writers narrate and political orators recount from their platforms are not only meanings that structure our sense of history, of how we came to be as a movement and as a community, but also theories of social change and strategies about how to end our oppression.

The lessons attributed to Stonewall are probably as numerous as the people for whom Stonewall is a symbol. But there are a few paradigmatic ones that recur endlessly. Like the snakes that St. Patrick drove out of Ireland, they figure prominently in our collective psyche:

- *Stonewall came out of the blue and started everything.* Before Stonewall there was naked oppression. After Stonewall, freedom beckoned.
- *Spontaneous riots and street action are the necessary keys to social change.* The raw anger erupting that night marks the path we need to follow.
- *The most oppressed will lead the way.* Because the young street people and the Puerto Rican drag queens who fought the police had nothing to lose, only they could take the risks that a freedom movement requires.

I mention these three because they are the ones I hear most often repeated and because they are almost completely untrue. They distort the past out of recognition, they elevate to preeminence an incomplete strategy for social change, and they become a weapon used within the community to discredit movement leaders. Each needs to be examined critically.

## Stonewall Started Everything

Pure and simple, Stonewall did *not* start everything. For almost twenty years before, some gay men and lesbians were organizing for freedom. By 1969, when the Stonewall Riot occurred, their efforts had contributed to changing the context in which gays and lesbians lived. For instance, through sustained lobbying, activists had won the support of the American Civil Liberties Union for sodomy law repeal, equal employment policies, and due process. This meant help in court when someone challenged federal employment policies; it meant access to skilled lawyers who could command media attention when police victimized the community with bar raids and mass arrests. Activists had also opened a dialogue with liberal ministers in many Protestant denominations and were working with sympathetic mental health professionals to contest the disease classification of homosexuality.

Because of the courage of these activists, gay life was not as grim as it had been. Their willingness to publish gay and lesbian magazines had led the Supreme Court to declare in 1958 that homosexuality did not constitute obscenity. By the 1960s, images of gay life were beginning to proliferate in mainstream media and culture. The challenges of these early activists to law enforcement practices meant that, in some states, gay bars were less likely arbitrarily to be shut down by the state, and in cities like New York and San Francisco, police harassment had been somewhat curtailed.

By the late 1960s, a few thousand women and men were involved in movement organizations, and a few hundred could be said to have come out of the closet. Their actions were becoming more militant and visible. On the East Coast, activists picketed the White House, the Pentagon, the Civil Service Commission, and the State Department. On the West Coast, they held public press conferences against police brutality and distributed leaflets at the California State Fair. In Los Angeles, activists were speaking out boldly and holding street demonstrations against police raids on gay bars. The community's new sense of confidence was reflected in the founding of the Metropolitan Community Church and the launching of [the gay magazine] the *Advocate*, the gay magazine both of whose births preceded Stonewall. The San Francisco community had faced its major confrontation with the police more than five years before Stonewall. It emboldened and aroused the community, and by the late 1960s local politicians were soliciting the votes of homosexuals. In the months before Stonewall, gay activism in the Bay Area was taking a decidedly more militant, radical, and "post-Stonewall" turn.

We are also learning, from the work of historians, that all sorts of incidents of resistance occurred before Stonewall. Participants may not have interpreted their acts as "political," and most likely did not think of themselves as "activists." But their deeds did enter the collective memory, the group consciousness of the lesbian and gay world. Whether displayed through the tough fighting spirit of bar dykes, or the sassy tongue of a piss-elegant queen, resistance was a part of the everyday life of the pre-Stonewall generation.

Stonewall, as I said, did not start everything. In fact, I think one can—and should—make the plausible argument that a street riot in

New York could lead to the flowering of a gay liberation movement precisely because the soil had been fertilized and the seeds planted by the preceding generation. Had a riot such as Stonewall occurred ten years earlier, not much would have come of it, and we probably would not commemorate it. With riots as with so much of life, timing is everything.

## Riots and Street Actions Are the Keys

Rioting and street demonstrations can be a lot of fun: I have participated in many in my decades as an activist. In certain circumstances, they have the power to galvanize people, crystallize sentiment, reveal discontent, and expose injustice. In other circumstances, they are a big dud. They can alienate outsiders, solidify the opposition, polarize a community, and mobilize the superior police power of the state. But in every case, a riot or a street action is nothing but an event—unless people choose to do something else after the rioting is over.

We already have other examples in our recent history of riots and street demonstrations. Some contributed to movement building; others led nowhere. The White Night riots in San Francisco in 1979 galvanized the community into further organizing and made it a more powerful force in the life and politics of San Francisco. Not long after that, gays in New York rioted for several nights to protest the making of the film *Cruising*. Not much came of it, and the New York movement in the early 1980s remained fractured and ineffective. In 1979, gay and lesbian activists called for a March on Washington; the turnout was not very large, and the results were disappointing. In 1987, a second march drew over half a million and led to an upsurge in grassroots organizing around the country. Many ACT UP chapters have used direct action and street activity to great effect; by contrast, many Queer Nation groups have employed similiar tactics, but have little to show for it.

Whether we realize it or not, the reason we commemorate Stonewall today is because, *after the rioting*, many gay men and lesbians chose to do something—organize. They moved from spontaneity to planned, intentional activity. Rather than wait for the police to come to them and provoke another outburst of anger, they formed organizations in order to engage in sustained activism. The first of the post-Stonewall groups in New York City was the Gay Liberation Front, an organization with a wide variety of members, but with a preponderance of people who identified with and were part of the radical movements of the 1960s. Around the country, GLFs formed, as did other kinds of gay, lesbian, and transgender organizations. The impetus for organizing often came from seeing a gay liberation banner or contingent at antiwar rallies and peace demonstrations. Other young radicals who were gay or lesbian returned from those events to form their own organizations.

In the first years after Stonewall, street demonstrations were a frequent and integral part of the gay liberation movement. The police and the media were often the targets. But these demonstrations required planning, discussion, and coordination: they didn't simply erupt spontaneously. Meanwhile, much of the work of gay liberation was far more mundane. Activists spoke in high school civics classes and college sociology courses. They formed caucuses in their professional associations and unions, and campaigned for visibility and job protection. They attended religious services as openly gay men and lesbians, met with ministers and priests and rabbis, and sought inclusion in these mainstream institutions. They lobbied for legislation, campaigned for progay candidates, and "zapped" homophobic ones. Some were part of the unspontaneous and unglamorous activity of litigation—filing suit in court to challenge discriminatory practices.

I am not privileging one form of activism over another. I do not believe marches are preferable to court cases, street riots preferable to testimony before a city council—or the reverse. The far-reaching revolutionary change that I yearn for will come about because we are flexible enough to use a broad spectrum of tactics and wise enough to develop a sound, long-range strategy. We will form organizations, support them, build them into powerful vehicles to advance our goals, and have the stamina to engage in the long march through institutions that liberation will require. When anger erupts into rioting, as it no doubt will again and again, we will know how to respond so that future Stonewalls likewise do not remain simply events, but become the building blocks of a just society.

## The Most Oppressed Will Lead the Way

Of all the myths associated with Stonewall, this one packs the most polemical power when it is used. It has become a battering ram, wielded to attack the credibility, motivation, and worth of many movement leaders, to whom the phrases "self-appointed" or "self-proclaimed" are generally attached as modifiers. Especially since the early 1980s, as some of our community organizations have grown prosperous enough to pay middle-class salaries, the men and women who fill these slots have often faced criticism not because of what they believe or do, but because of who they are—the possessors of some of the privileges that an exploitative society parsimoniously dishes out.

"Privilege" is not, in itself, either a good or a bad thing. The problem with privilege—in income, education, housing, and the like—is not that some people have it, but that most don't. In a society stratified by gender, race, and class hierarchies, the material elements of a good life become accidents of birth or circumstance. The critical issue ought to be how one uses privilege: to perpetuate oppression and inequality or to challenge it. This is a political question, best answered by examining someone's words and deeds. Attacking leaders simply because of their identity, or simply because they occupy a prominent place in the organizational structure of the movement, makes no sense. It is destructive and harmful, an example of misplaced resentment.

The assumption that privilege makes one politically suspect or somehow inadequate as an agent of social change also threatens to obscure the truth at the heart of our movement: *All* homosexuals are oppressed; gay oppression is real and vicious. It isn't necessary to shed extra tears for the plight of prosperous white gay men in order to acknowledge that if one scratches below the surface of any gay life, one will find a bottomless well of pain whose source is oppression. And gays with privilege risk their status and expose themselves to penalties when they make the leap to activism.

To question the statement that "the most oppressed will lead the way" is *not* to argue for the inverse of that proposition. An authentic liberation movement must articulate the needs of everyone. The varied configurations of privilege and oppression that exist among us pose an enormous challenge in agenda setting. We will rise to that challenge only when the movement has incorporated the aspirations of the most oppressed. This is a political question whose answer is not perfectly correlated to identity. Oppression does not necessarily spawn political virtue or wisdom; privilege does not necessarily compromise integrity.

I marched in my first Stonewall Day parade in 1973. It was a gloriously bright day in New York. Like the buds that swell under the light of the spring sun, I could feel myself ready to burst with happiness as I strode through the streets of Manhattan, my arms linked with those of my friends. Years and years of gay freedom day marches have not diminished that feeling.

Stonewall will remain a symbol of prideful resistance as long as gay and lesbian oppression survives. Let's embrace the symbol and dispense with the myths.

# CHAPTER 2

# GAY AND LESBIAN FAMILIES

# THE RISE OF THE GAY FAMILY

Dan Gilgoff

More children are being raised by gay or lesbian parents in the
United States than ever before. In this selection Dan Gilgoff
reports that gay- and lesbian-headed families are settling in every
area of the country—urban, suburban, and rural—and many live
in the most culturally conservative states in the country, such as
Mississippi, South Dakota, Alaska, South Carolina, and Louisiana.
While new support networks for gay families have developed in a
few states, such as Vermont and Massachusetts, little support is
available for families in conservative settings that limit the rights
of same-sex parents. In spite of such hurdles, more gays and lesbians are having children and challenging traditional notions of
the American family. Dan Gilgoff is a reporter for *U.S. News &
World Report.*

"We were afraid people out here would be skeptical of us," says Sheri
Ciancia, sipping a glass of iced tea outside the four-bedroom house she
and her partner bought last fall in Tomball, Texas, a half-hour's drive
from Houston. "Afraid they wouldn't let their kids play with ours."

"But we've got to take chances," adds Stephanie Caraway, Ciancia's
partner of seven years, sitting next to her on their concrete patio as
their 8-year-old daughter, Madison, attempts to break her own record
for consecutive bounces on a pogo stick. "We're not going to live in
fear."

A trio of neighborhood boys pedal their bikes up the driveway, say
hello to the moms, and ask Madison if they can use her bike ramp.
The boys cruise up and down the ramp's shallow slopes while Madison continues bouncing, the picture of suburban serenity. Despite
their misgivings about relocating from Houston to this tidy subdivi-
sion, the family has yet to encounter hostility from their neighbors.
"We have to give straight people more credit," Caraway says with a
wry smile. "I'm working on that."

Tomball—its roads lined with single-room Baptist churches and the
occasional sprawling worship complex, known to some locals as
"Jesus malls"—may seem an unlikely magnet for gay couples raising

kids. A year before Caraway and Ciancia moved here, activists in the neighboring county got a popular children's book that allegedly "tries to minimize or even negate that homosexuality is a problem" temporarily removed from county libraries. So imagine Caraway's and Ciancia's surprise when, shortly after moving in, their daughter met another pair of moms rollerblading down their block: a lesbian couple who had moved into the neighborhood with their kids just a few months earlier.

## The Nature of the American Family

Gay families have arrived in suburban America, in small-town America, in Bible Belt America—in all corners of the country. According to the latest census data, there are now more than 160,000 families with two gay parents and roughly a quarter of a million children spread across some 96 percent of U.S. counties. That's not counting the kids being raised by single gay parents, whose numbers are likely much higher—upwards of a million, by most estimates, though such households aren't tracked.

[On May 17, 2004], the commonwealth of Massachusetts recharged the gay-marriage debate by becoming the first state to offer marriage licenses to same-sex couples. The move has raised the ire of conservatives who believe gay marriage tears at the fabric of society—and earned support from progressives who think gay men and lesbians deserve the same rights as heterosexuals. But the controversy is not simply over the bond between two men or two women; it's about the very nature of the American family.

Gay parents say their families are much like those led by their straight counterparts. "I just say I have two moms," says Madison, explaining how she tells friends about her parents (whom she refers to as "Mom" and "Mamma Sheri"). "They're no different from other parents except that they're two girls. It's not like comparing two parents with two trees. It's comparing two parents with two other parents."

Many of today's gay parents, who grew up with few gay-parent role models, say their efforts have helped introduce a culture of family to the gay community. "In the straight community, adoption is a secondary choice," says Rob Calhoun, 35, who adopted a newborn daughter with his partner 20 months ago. "But in the gay community, it's like, 'Wow, you've achieved the ultimate American dream.'"

The dream has not been without cost, though. Gay parents and their kids in many parts of the country frequently meet with friction from the outside world, in the form of scornful family members, insensitive classmates, and laws that treat same-sex parents differently from straight parents. In general, Americans are split on the subject. A [2004] national poll . . . found that 45 percent believe gays should have the right to adopt; 47 percent do not.

Many traditional-marriage advocates argue that marriage is first and foremost about procreation. "It is the reason for marriage," Pennsylvania Sen. Rick Santorum said [in 2003]. "Marriage is not about affirming somebody's love for somebody else. It's about uniting together to be open to children." Other critics call gay and lesbian couples who are raising kids—whether from previous marriages, adoption, or artificial insemination—dangerously self-centered. "It's putting adult desires above the interest of children," says Bill Maier, psychologist in residence at [research institute] Focus on the Family and coauthor of . . . *Marriage on Trial: The Case Against Same-Sex Marriage and Parenting.* "For the first time in history, we're talking about intentionally creating permanently motherless and fatherless families."

## Evidence?

Three decades of social science research has supplied some ammunition for both sides of the gay-parent debate. Many researchers say that while children do best with two parents, the stability of the parents' relationship is much more important than their gender. The American Psychological Association, the American Academy of Pediatrics, the National Association of Social Workers, and the American Bar Association have all released statements condoning gay parenting. "Not a single study has found a difference [between children of gay and straight parents] that you can construe as harmful," says Judith Stacey, a professor of sociology, gender, and sexuality at New York University and a gay-rights advocate.

Stacey and other researchers even suggest that gay and lesbian parents who form families through adoption, artificial insemination, or surrogacy may offer some advantages over straight parents. "In the lesbian and gay community, parents are a self-selecting group whose motivation for parenthood is high," says Charlotte Patterson, a psychologist and researcher at the University of Virginia. But studies on the subject have so far examined relatively few children (fewer than 600, by some counts) and virtually no kids of gay dads.

One study coauthored by Stacey and widely cited by both supporters and opponents of gay parenting found that children of lesbians are mere likely to consider homosexual relationships themselves (though no more likely to identify as homosexuals as adults) and less likely to exhibit gender-stereotyped behavior. "If we could break down some of society's gender stereotypes, that would be a good thing," says Ellen Perrin, professor of pediatrics at the Floating Hospital for Children at Tufts-New England Medical Center. Focus on the Family's Maier disagrees: "They don't have rigid gender stereotypes? That's gender identity confusion."

While the debate continues, the number of kids with gay parents keeps growing. According to Gary Gates, an Urban Institute demographer, 1 in 3 lesbian couples was raising children in 2000, up from 1 in 5 in 1990, while the number of male couples raising kids jumped from 1 in 20 to 1 in 5 during the same period. The uptick is partly due to changes in the census itself, which in 1990 tabulated most same-sex couples that identified themselves as married on census forms as straight married couples. In the 2000 census, though, those couples were tabulated as gay and lesbian partners. But the leap in such couples with children is large enough to suggest a real spike. And because gay and lesbian couples are sometimes reluctant to identify themselves as such on census forms, actual figures could be much higher.

## Moving In

What's perhaps most surprising is that gay- and lesbian-headed families are settling in some of the most culturally conservative parts of the country. According to the Gay and Lesbian Atlas, published earlier this month by the Urban Institute, Alaska, Arizona, Georgia, Louisiana, and New Mexico are among the 10 states with the largest number of gay families—along with more historically gay-friendly New York, California, and Vermont. States where gay and lesbian couples are most likely to have children (relative to the state's total number of gay couples) are Mississippi, South Dakota, Alaska, South Carolina, and Louisiana, in that order. "Same-sex couples who live in areas where all couples are more likely to have children" may simply be more likely to have children themselves, according to the atlas. And couples with children—regardless of their sexual orientation—are looking for good schools, safe streets, and outdoor green space. "It's gay couples who don't have kids whose behavior tends to be different: They live in more-distressed areas of cities, with higher crime and more racial diversity," says Gates. "But a large portion of gay people own their homes, live in the suburbs, and are raising two children."

Most of these children are the products of previous heterosexual relationships. Madison, for one, is Caraway's daughter by a former boyfriend. Caraway says the pregnancy forced her to come to terms with her homosexuality; she started dating Ciancia soon after her daughter's birth. "If you stay in a relationship but you're not in love or committed to the person, children sense that," says Caraway, now 31. "What kind of message does that send?"

But as these children enter middle and high school, their peers are more likely to inquire about their parents' sexuality—and not always politely. The Tufts-New England Medical Center's Perrin, who authored the American Academy of Pediatrics' policy on gay parenting, says that children of same-sex parents "get stigmatized because of who their parents are. It's the biggest problem they face by far." Just like many gays and lesbians themselves, children of homosexuals speak of "coming out" as a long and often difficult ordeal. "You are, on a day-to-day basis, choosing if you're out or if you're going to be hiding the whole truth," says Abigail Garner, author of the recently released *Families Like*

*Mine*, about children of homosexuals. "Is she your mom's roommate or your aunt or your mom's friend?"

During middle school and part of high school, A.J. Costa, now a freshman at Texas Lutheran University outside San Antonio, kept his mother's relationship with a live-in partner secret. He grew close to his mom's partner, even preferred the arrangement to his mom's previous marriage, which ended when he was 7, but never invited friends to the house. "I didn't want anyone to make fun of me," says Costa. "Nobody was going to mess with my family."

Costa's fears were reinforced by some classmates who did find out and referred to his moms as "dykes." But in the summer before his junior year in high school, Costa visited Provincetown, Mass., for "Family Week," an annual gathering of gay parents and their children. "I couldn't get over how many families there were, all like mine," he recalls. "I realized that it wasn't about whether I have two gay moms. It was that I have two moms. It was getting past the fact that they're gay."

## Support Networks

In recent years, support networks for children of gay parents and for parents themselves have expanded dramatically. Children of Lesbians and Gays Everywhere, or COLAGE, has chapters in 28 states. The Family Pride Coalition, whose dozens of local affiliate organizations attract gay parents who want their kids to meet other children of gays and lesbians, has doubled its member and volunteer base in the past five years, to 17,000. Vacation companies like Olivia, founded 30 years ago for lesbian travelers, now offer packages specifically for gays and lesbians with children, and R Family Vacations, underwritten by former talk-show host Rosie O'Donnell, will launch its inaugural cruise this summer. Tanya Voss, a 36-year-old college professor in Austin who, with her partner, has two young boys through artificial insemination, plans to attend the first Family Pride Coalition weekend at Disney World next month. Kids need environments where "they don't have to explain their families," she says, "a safe place where they could just be."

Still, neither COLAGE nor Family Pride Coalition has affiliate groups in Mississippi, South Dakota, or Alaska, the states where gay and lesbian couples are most likely to have kids. ("The way you manage in a more hostile environment," says Gates, "is to go about your business and not draw much attention to yourself.") Many such states also present the highest legal hurdles for those families. Roughly two thirds of children with same-sex parents live in states where second-parent or joint adoptions—which allow the partner of a child's biological or adoptive parent to adopt that child without stripping the first parent of his or her rights, much like stepparent adoption—has been granted only in certain counties or not at all.

Absent such arrangements, a biological or adoptive parent's partner could be powerless to authorize emergency medical treatment or denied custody if the other parent dies. When Voss and her partner were planning to have their first child, they decided Voss wouldn't carry the baby because her parents—who disapprove of Voss's homosexuality—would have likely claimed custody in the event that their daughter died during childbirth.

Gay-rights advocates argue that it's often children who end up suffering from laws restricting gay parenting—and same-sex marriage. If a parent without a legal relationship with his or her partner's child dies, a 10-year-old child whose nonlegal parent was earning $60,000 at the time of death, for example, would forgo nearly $140,000 in Social Security survivor benefits paid to children of married couples, according to the Urban Institute and the Human Rights Campaign. That's on top of the more than $100,000 in Social Security paid to a widow—but not a gay partner—whose spouse earned $60,000. And without laws recognizing them as legitimate parents, nonlegal parents are unlikely to be required to pay child support if they leave their partner.

Recently, some states have further restricted adoption. Earlier [in 2004], a federal appeals court upheld Florida's ban on homosexuals' adopting children, the only one of its kind in the nation. Arkansas now bans gay foster parenting, Mississippi bans same-sex couples from adopting, and Utah bans adoptions by all unmarried couples. "State legislatures that opposed gay marriage are going to push to replicate what Florida has done," says lawyer John Mayoue, author of *Balancing Competing Interests in Family Law.* "We'll see more of this as part of the backlash against gay marriage."

Even so, more gay couples—especially male couples—are adopting than ever before. A [2003] study found that 60 percent of adoption agencies accept applications from homosexuals, up from just a few a decade ago. The 2000 census showed that 26 percent of gay male couples with children designate a stay-at-home parent, compared with 25 percent of straight parents. "When you have children, whether you're gay or straight, you spend lots of time wondering how good a job you're doing for your kids; you lose sleep over it," says Mark Brown, 49, whose partner stays home with their two young adopted kids. "It doesn't leave much time to worry about how we're being perceived by straight society."

# Legalizing Gay Adoption Will Give Children More Stable Lives

E.J. Graff

The majority of Americans are ambivalent about the idea of lesbians and gay men raising children. As a result, the legal system is not consistent in its rulings about gay and lesbian adoption. As E.J. Graff describes in the following viewpoint, when a lesbian couple has a baby, the biological mother has the legal rights to the child. It is up to the courts to decide whether the mother's partner can also assume the legal rights of guardian. Judges in half of the states have allowed "second-parent adoption," but in only seven of the states is it a statewide policy. In the other states, the legal decisions of judges are unpredictable. In one county a judge might rule in favor of second-parent adoption, while in another a judge might rule against it. Graff argues that gay adoption needs to be legalized in all states in order to provide a stable family life for children. Without two legally recognized parents, she states, children face potentially disruptive and painful situations. For example, if the biological mother dies, the biological grandparents may attempt to challenge the guardianship of the co-mom and fight for custody of the child. In addition, because the laws about second-parent adoption vary from state to state, gay and lesbian parents who relocate or simply travel to another area risk having their legal status as guardians revoked. Graff also argues that despite arguments to the contrary, studies show that children raised by gay and lesbian parents have normal emotional, intellectual, moral, and social development. E.J. Graff is an author and journalist who has written extensively on same-sex marriage and related issues.

Imagine waking up one morning to the news that because of a recent court decision, you may no longer be your child's legal parent. Forget all those times you've read *Goodnight Moon*, those long nights you

E.J. Graff, "The Other Marriage War," *American Prospect*, vol. 13, April 8, 2002. Copyright © 2002 by *American Prospect*, 5 Broad St., Boston, MA 02109. Reproduced by permission.

spent in a steam-filled bathroom trying to keep your sick child breathing. In the eyes of the law, you may suddenly be just a kind stranger. No emergency room, insurance plan, schoolteacher, tax man, or judge will count you as essential to your child.

Sound like one of Kafka's nightmares? It's what happened to thousands of California parents last October [2001], when a San Diego court struck down the procedure by which, for 15 years, lesbian co-mothers—parents who helped to imagine, create, feed, clothe, and raise a child, but who didn't give birth—had legally adopted their children. Many California lawyers' phones rang nonstop until the decision was erased from the books while it went up on appeal.[1]

Welcome to the world of lesbian and gay parents, where you can be a parent one day and not the next; in one state but not another; when you're straight but not when you're gay. At any moment, your heterosexual ex might find a judge willing to yank the kids after you come out. Or you might hear your parental fitness debated by strangers—on radio, on TV, and in newspapers—using language that makes your children wake up at night from dreams that the government has taken you away.

Yes, the climate for lesbian and gay parents has improved dramatically in the past 20 years. There can't be an American left who hasn't heard about Heather and her two mommies. And though the children's book by that name kicked off an antigay uproar in the early 1990s, by the end of the decade the mainstream media were covering [famous lesbians] Melissa Etheridge and Julie Cypher's two babies without a blink. . . . The lesbian baby boom began in Boston and San Francisco in the mid-1980s. In both cities, after mainstream doctors refused to offer donor insemination (DI) services to unmarried women, lesbians started their own sperm banks and DI clinics. Since then, two-mom families have popped up everywhere from Maine to Utah, from Alaska to Florida. In smaller numbers, gay dads have followed, taking in foster children, hiring surrogates, or adopting (as individuals, if necessary) whenever they could find birth moms, local authorities, or judges who'd help. And that's only the latest incarnation of gay and lesbian parenting. Lesbians and gay men have long become parents the conventional way: through heterosexual marriage.

But law is lagging badly behind this social transformation. Although many [people] . . . may know two-mom or two-dad families, they probably do not know about the daily legal insecurity, the extra level of anxiety and effort, and the occasional shocking injustices those families face. Society is still profoundly ambivalent about lesbians and gay men—and about the unfamiliar, sometimes queasy-

---

1. The California Supreme Court reversed the lower court's decision in August 2003, affirming the validity of second-parent adoptions.

making idea of queers raising kids. As a result, unpredictable legal decisions about lesbian and gay parents too often leave their children in limbo.

## The Children Turn Out Just Fine

Is there any reason to worry about how these kids are raised? No. More than 20 studies have been done on about 300 children of lesbians and gay men. Some compare children of divorced lesbian moms or gay dads with children of divorced heterosexual moms or dads; others compare two-mom families with mom-and-pop families that used the same DI clinic. The results are quite clear: Children of lesbian or gay parents turn out just fine on every conceivable measure of emotional and social development: attachment, self-esteem, moral judgment, behavior, intelligence, likability, popularity, gender identity, family warmth, and all sorts of obscure psychological concepts. Whatever the scale, children with lesbian or gay parents and children with heterosexual parents turn out equally well—and grow up to be heterosexual in the same overwhelming proportions.

Not surprisingly, antigay pundits challenge this conclusion. Brigham Young University law professor Lynn Wardle and his followers argue that the population samples in these studies have been exceedingly small, haven't been "randomly" chosen, and don't accurately represent lesbian and gay parents as a whole. All these charges are accurate, as far as they go. But the conclusion drawn by Wardle and company—that the results are therefore meaningless—is not. Here's the problem: No one can ever get a "random" sample of lesbians or gay men, much less of lesbian or gay *parents*, so long as there's any stigma to being gay—and any realistic fear that the children might be taken away. For the most part, researchers have had to make do with samples of lesbian or gay parents who will consent to being studied and match them with groups of heterosexual parents. Does that limitation invalidate these studies? Maybe it would if results varied dramatically, but because they are remarkably consistent, the vast majority of social scientists and physicians accept them. Social science deals with people, not elements on the periodic table. Like doctors, they must always make informed decisions based on the best and latest evidence.

That's why organizations such as the American Psychological Association, the National Association of Social Workers, the American Academy of Child and Adolescent Psychiatry, and the American Counseling Association have released statements in support of lesbian and gay parents. This February [2002], for instance, the American Academy of Pediatrics [AAP] came out with a report that had been vetted by an unprecedented number of committees and had taken four years to wend its way toward the academy's full approval. Its conclusion: "No data have pointed to any risk to children as a result of growing up in a family with one or more gay parents." Nor, the AAP found, is parents' sexual orientation an important variable in how kids turn out.

So what is? If basics like food, shelter, clothing, and health care are covered, what matters to kids is the happiness and satisfaction of the parents. Are the parents happily mated and content with the way household responsibilities are shared? Or are they miserable and sniping at each other, whether together or separated? You can guess which type of household will produce happier and more confident kids. Harmony helps children; conflict and disruption hurt. Despite the yammering of the conservative marriage movement, *how* households are run matters more than *who* (read: which sex or sexual orientation) runs them.

## Differences Are Not Necessarily Bad

There's another right-wing line of challenge to these studies: shouting about statistical blips. Occasionally, intriguing differences do show up between the children of lesbian moms and those of heterosexual moms. Here, conservatives want it both ways: They want to throw out the common findings because of methodological suspicions while making a big deal about onetime results. But in every case, these variations are differences, not deficits. For instance, in one study of kids with divorced moms, the lesbians' daughters were more comfortable than the heterosexual women's daughters in "rough-and-tumble" play, more likely to play with trucks and guns—although the sons were no more likely to play with tea sets or Barbies. More controversially, a British study found that more of the divorced lesbians' children said that they had imagined or tried a same-sex romance; but as adults, they still called themselves straight or gay in the same proportions as the straight moms' kids. Is it good, bad, or neutral that lesbians might raise their children to feel free to try out all sides of themselves in gender and sexuality? Or are these results too small to be generalized? The answers depend on your political point of view. And in a pluralist society, that must be taken as an argument for freedom of choice in child-rearing.

## The Need for Stability

So what do these children need from society? The same thing all children need: clear and enforceable ties to their parents. Child psychologist Anna Freud once wrote that children "can handle almost anything better than instability." Not coincidentally, trying to shore up a family's stability is the goal of much marriage-and-family law.

Except if your parents are gay. . . . If a map were to be drawn of the legal situation for lesbian and gay parents, it would look kaleidoscopic . . . with the colors constantly shifting. The answers to some questions may be predictable by geography. On others, even in the supposedly liberal states, how well you're treated depends on your judge. . . .

Things are even iffier for two-mom families than for divorced parents who come out. Most judges just don't know what to do with these families. Adoption laws, written by state legislatures in the late nineteenth century, cover two situations: a couple adopting an orphan or a remarried parent who wants legally to link the child to the stepparent. A mother can add a father; a father can add a mother. But can a mother add *another* mother? Most judges say no, with attitudes ranging from uncertainty to outright antagonism; one Illinois judge, Susan McDunn, went so far as to appoint the Family Research Council [a conservative Christian advocacy group] as *guardian ad litem*[2] for the children. Judges in up to half the states have allowed what's called "second-parent adoption," but in only seven states and the District of Columbia is this a statewide policy. Elsewhere, you're playing roulette: In Michigan, for instance, an Ann Arbor judge might grant one, while a Grand Rapids judge might say no. And advocates try not to appeal—because of the risk that the appeals court might flatly rule out second-parent adoptions, as has happened in the Wisconsin supreme court and in five other states' appellate courts. . . .

No biggie, some people think: Just write a will and some health care proxies, appoint a guardian, and you're all set. It's not that simple. The biomom better be the breadwinner, because the co-mom won't be able to list the child on her taxes or health insurance; nor can she pass on her Social Security benefits or pension. If the biomom dies, the biological grandparents can challenge the co-mom's guardianship and legally kidnap the child. And if the moms break up, cross your fingers for that child.

## Custody Battle Nightmares

Many—one hopes most—divorcing couples put aside their anger to do what's best for their children. Not everyone does. We all know how hideous people can be when fighting over custody: They play dirty, cheat, lie, even kidnap, always persuading themselves that they're doing it for the kids. When lesbian couples have such no-holds-barred breakups, a spiteful biomom can pull legal rank. If the facts won't let her eviscerate her ex's right to custody or visitation, she may insist that the co-mom was never a parent at all, but just a babysitter, a visitor, a pretender, a stalker. (Because gay men don't give birth, they more often start out on an equal legal footing and can't use this trick.) A biomom and her attorney may exploit a judge's discomfort with homosexuality or cite the state's Defense of Marriage Act to blowtorch any legal link between the co-mom and the child. And if the biomom wins, it leaves tortuous and cruel case law on the

2. A *guardian ad litem* is a special guardian appointed by the court to represent the child's interests in a particular litigation.

state's books that can hurt other lesbian and gay families for decades.

These cases can be heartbreaking. There's the video of the moms' wedding, there's the co-mom's last name as the child's middle name, there's the Olan Mills picture of the three together—and there's the biomom in court saying, "Keep that dyke away from my child." How gratuitously nasty—and legally dangerous—can it be? After getting a legal second-parent adoption in Illinois, one couple moved to Florida to take care of the biomom's dying mother. There the pair broke up. Florida has the dubious distinction of hosting the nation's most draconian ban on adoptions by lesbians and gay men. And so in court, the biomom is now arguing that Florida should refuse to recognize her ex's "foreign" adoption of the child. If this biomom wins, every other two-mom or two-dad family will have to think thrice about visiting Key West or Disney World: What if a Florida emergency room or police station refused to recognize their adoption?

Similar cases are percolating in Nebraska and North Carolina. If these biomoms win, the map of the United States could become a checkerboard of states where two-mom and two-dad families don't dare travel. Can you imagine having your parenthood dissolve when you hit the interstate? You might never leave home again.

"This is a level of damage," says Kendell of the National Center for Lesbian Rights, "that [conservatives] Jerry Falwell and Pat Robertson and Lou Sheldon and all their ilk can only dream of."

## More Courts Are Recognizing Gay and Lesbian Parents

Coherent laws and public policies are desperately needed to help gay and lesbian parents order their families' lives. Fortunately, history's heading in the right direction. More and more state courts are coming up with guidelines that refuse to let a biomom shut out her ex, or a co-mom skip out on child support, if the pair together planned for and reared their child. The public and the media are sympathetic. Most policy makers are open to persuasion, understanding that even if they wouldn't want to be gay themselves, kids whose parents are gay deserve the most security possible.

Unfortunately, lesbian-gay-bisexual-transgender advocacy organizations can't change the legal landscape alone. Both in the courts and in public opinion, gay folks are too often cast as biased, the mirror image of the radical right. As a result, liberals and progressives—especially heterosexuals—can make an enormous difference in the lives of these families.

"Children who are born to or adopted by one member of a same-sex couple deserve the security of two legally recognized parents," reads the February [2002] report from the American Academy of Pediatrics. Originally written to be an amicus brief for co-moms or co-dads trying to sway a judge into waving the parent-making wand, the AAP report did much more: It gave editorial writers and talk shows across the country an excuse to agree. And aside from *The Washington Times* and press-release attacks from the usual suspects, agree they did, in an astonishing array of news outlets ranging from local radio shows to *USA Today* to *The Columbus Dispatch*.

So what, besides social tolerance, should the forces of good be working for? Policies and laws that tie these kids firmly to their real, daily parents. These children need strong statutes that let co-moms and co-dads adopt—preferably without the intrusive home study, the thousands of dollars in legal fees, and the reference letters from colleagues and friends that are now required. They need decisive guidelines saying that an adoption in one state is an adoption in every state. And they need marriage rights for their parents. Much of marriage law is designed to help spouses rear families, letting them make a single shelter from their combined incomes, assets, benefits, pensions, habits, strengths, weaknesses, and knowledge. Today, when a heterosexual married couple uses DI, the man is automatically the legal father (as long as he has consented in writing) without having to adopt; if any marriage (or even some lesser system of recognition, like civil unions or registered partnership) were possible, the same could and should be true for lesbians.

By taking up this banner, liberals and progressives can prove that they have a practical commitment to real families and real children. As an Ontario judge wrote in 1995: "When one reflects on the seemingly limitless parade of neglected, abandoned and abused children who appear before our courts in protection cases daily, all of whom have been in the care of heterosexual parents in a 'traditional' family structure, the suggestion that it might not ever be in the best interests of these children to be raised by loving, caring, and committed parents who might happen to be lesbian or gay, is nothing short of ludicrous."

# GAY ADOPTION PUTS CHILDREN AT RISK

Paul Cameron

The American Academy of Pediatrics (AAP) published a report in 2000 that advocated the adoption of children by gay and lesbian parents. They also stated that "growing up with parents who are lesbian or gay may confer some advantages to children." According to research psychologist Paul Cameron, in promoting adoption by homosexual parents, the AAP ignored the data about the many problems children raised by gay and lesbian parents face, including the risk of molestation, domestic violence, and psychological problems. Cameron also argues that gays and lesbians have a much lower life expectancy than heterosexuals and that it is therefore unfair to allow the adoption of children to parents who might not be there to raise them until they reach adulthood. The AAP and other gay rights activists are more interested in promoting their agenda for "gay rights" than in considering the best interests of children, Cameron concludes. Paul Cameron is the chairman of the Family Research Institute and author of *The Gay 90s: What the Empirical Evidence Reveals About Homosexuality.*

On Feb. 4, 2000, the American Academy of Pediatrics (AAP) recommended "legal and legislative efforts" to allow children "born to or adopted by one member of a gay or lesbian couple" to be adopted by the homosexual partner. Such a law effectively would eliminate the possibility of adoption by other family members following the death of the parent. It also would cause problems for numerous children.

The AAP, like many other professional organizations, apparently was too caught up in promoting identity politics to address all the evidence relevant to homosexual adoption. In its report, the organization offered only positive evidence about gays and lesbians as parents. "In fact," the report concluded, "growing up with parents who are lesbian or gay may confer some advantages to children." Really?

There are three sets of information on the issue: clinical reports of psychiatric disturbance of children with homosexual parents, testimonies of children with homosexual parents concerning their situation and studies that have compared the children of homosexuals with the children of nonhomosexuals. The AAP ignored the first two sets and had to cherry-pick the comparative studies to arrive at the claim that "[n]o data have pointed to any risk to children as a result of growing up in a family with one or more gay parents."

## The Problems of Children with Homosexual Parents

A number of clinical reports detail "acting-out behavior," homosexual seduction, elective muteness and the desire for a mother by children with homosexual parents. I am unaware of a single child being disturbed because his mother and father were married.

The AAP also ignored the testimonies of children with homosexual parents—probably the best evidence since these kids had to "live with it" rather than deal with a theory. More than 150 children with homosexual parents have provided, in extensive interviews, detailed evidence of the difficulties they encountered as a result. A study Paul and Kirk Cameron published this year [2002] in *Psychological Reports* analyzed the content of 57 life-story narratives by children with homosexual parents assembled by lesbian researchers Louise Rafkin (United States) and Lisa Saffron (Britain).

In these narratives, children in 48 of the 52 families (92 percent) mentioned one or more "problems." Of the 213 problems which were scored—including hypersexuality, instability, molestation, domestic violence—children attributed 201 (94 percent) to their homosexual parent(s).

Here are four sample excerpts:

- One 9-year-old girl said: "My biological mother is S. and my other mother is L. We've lived together for a year. Before that L. lived across the street. . . . My mom met L.; L. had just broken up with someone. We moved in together because it got complicated going back and forth every night. All of a sudden I felt like I was a different person because my mom was a lesbian. . . . I get angry because I can't tell anybody about my mom. The kids at school would laugh. . . . They say awful things about lesbians . . . then they make fun of me. Having lesbian mothers is nothing to laugh about. . . . I have told my [mother] that she has made my life difficult."

- A 12-year-old boy in the United Kingdom said: "Mum . . . has had several girlfriends in my lifetime. . . . I don't go around saying that I've got two mums. . . . If we are sitting in a restaurant eating, she'll say, 'I want you to know about all these sex things.' And she'll go on about everything, just shouting it out. . . . Sometimes when mum embarrasses me, I think, 'I wish I had a dad.' . . . Been to every gay pride march. Last year, while attending, we went up to a field . . . when two men came up to us. One of them started touching me. I didn't want to go this year because of that."

- According to a 39-year-old woman: "In my memories, I'm always looking for my mother and finding her with a woman doing things I don't understand. . . . Sometimes they blame me for opening a door that wasn't even locked. . . . [At about the age of 10], I noticed a door that I hadn't yet opened. Inside I saw a big bed. My mother sat up suddenly and stared at me. She was with B. . . . and then B. shouted, 'You f***ing sneaking brat!' My mother never said a word. [Then came N.] I came to hate N. because of the way she and my mother fought every night. They screamed and bickered and whined and pouted over everything. N. closed my mother's hand in the car door. . . . She and N. hadn't made love in seven years."

- According to a 19-year-old man: "When I was about 7, my mother told me that this woman, D., was going to stay with us for a while—and she never left! I didn't think anything much about it until I was about 10. . . . It just became obvious because she and my mother were sleeping together. A few months after D. left, my mother started to see another woman, but that didn't last. Then she got involved with a different woman . . . ; she'd be violent toward my mother. . . . After that she started to go on marches and to women's groups. . . . There were some women in these groups who objected to men altogether, and I couldn't cope with that."

All 57 narratives can be found at www.familyresearchinst.org. Anyone who believes that living with homosexual parents confers "some advantages to children" should read these accounts.

## Studies Were Ignored

The AAP ignored every comparative study of children that showed those with homosexual parents experiencing more problems. These include the largest comparative study, reported in 1996 by Sotirios Sarantakos in the journal, *Children Australia*, of 58 elementary school-children raised by coupled homosexual parents who were closely matched (by age, sex, grade in school, social class) with 58 children of cohabiting heterosexual parents and 58 raised by married parents. Teachers reported that the married couples' children scored best at math and language but somewhat lower in social studies, experienced the highest level of parental involvement at school as well as at home and had parents with the highest expectations for them. The children of homosexuals scored lowest in math and language and somewhat higher in social studies, were the least popular, experienced the lowest level of parental involvement at school and at home, had parents with the lowest expectations for them and least frequently expressed higher educational and career expectations.

Yet the AAP said that studies have "failed to document any differences between such groups on . . . academic success." The organization's report also ignored the only empirical study based upon a random sample that reported on 17 adults (out of a sample of 5,182) with homosexual parents. Detailed by Cameron and Cameron in the journal *Adolescence* in 1996, the 17 were disproportionately apt to report sexual relations with their parents, more apt to report a less than exclusively heterosexual orientation, more frequently reported gender dissatisfaction and were more apt to report that their first sexual experience was homosexual.

The AAP report also seemingly ignored a 1998 *Psychological Reports* study by Cameron and Cameron that included the largest number of children with homosexual parents. That study compared 73 children of homosexuals with 105 children of heterosexuals. Of the 66 problems cited by panels of judges who extensively reviewed the living conditions and psychological reactions of children of homosexuals undergoing a divorce from heterosexuals, 64 (97 percent) were attributed to the homosexual parent.

Finally, while ignoring studies that contradicted its own conclusions, the AAP misrepresented numerous findings from the limited literature it cited. Thus, Sharon Huggins compared 18 children of 16 volunteer/lesbian mothers with 18 children of 16 volunteer/heterosexual/divorced mothers on self-esteem. Huggins reported statistically nonsignificant differences between the 19 children of mothers who were not living with a lover versus the 17 children of mothers who were living with a lover; and, further, that [the four] "adolescent daughters with high self-esteem had been told of their mother's lesbianism at a mean age of 6.0 years. In contrast, [the five] adolescent daughters with low self-esteem had been told at a mean age of 9.6 years" and "three of four of the mothers with high self-esteem daughters were currently living with lesbian lovers, but only one of four of the lesbian mothers with low self-esteem daughters was currently living with a lesbian lover."

The AAP cited Huggins as proving that "children's self-esteem has been shown to be higher among adolescents whose mothers (of any sexual orientation) were in a new partnered relationship after divorce, compared with those whose mother remained single, and among those who found out at a younger age that their parent was homosexual, compared with those who found out when they were older," thus transforming statistical nonevents based on niggling numbers of volunteers into important differences—twice in one sentence!

We have examined more than 10,000 obituaries of homosexuals: The median age of death for lesbians was in the 40s to 50s; for homosexuals it was in the 40s. Most Americans live into their 70s. Yet in the 1996 U.S. government sex survey the oldest lesbian was 49 years old and the oldest gay 54.

Children with homosexual parents are considerably more apt to lose a parent to death. Indeed, a homosexual couple in their 30s is roughly equivalent to a nonhomosexual couple in their late 40s or 50s. Adoption agencies will seldom permit a couple in their late 40s or 50s to adopt a child because of the risk of parental death, and the consequent social and psychological difficulty for the child. The AAP did not address this fact—one with profound implications for any child legally related to a homosexual.

## Gay Activists Are Manipulating Research

As usual, the media picked up on the AAP report as authoritative, assuming that it represented the consensus of a large and highly educated membership. Not so. As in other professional organizations, the vast majority of members pay their dues, read the journal and never engage in professional politics. As a consequence, a small but active minority of members gains control and uses the organization to promote its agenda. Too often, the result is ideological literature that misrepresents the true state of knowledge.

Gay-rights activists have been particularly adept at manipulating research and reports to their own ends. For years the media reported that all studies revealed that 10 percent of the population was homosexual. In fact, few if any studies ever came to that conclusion. For the next few years we will have to live with the repeated generalization that all studies prove homosexual parents are as good for children as heterosexual parents, and perhaps even better. What little literature exists on the subject proves no such thing. Indeed, translated into the language of accounting, the AAP report could be described as "cooking the books."

# THE CHILDREN OF GAY PARENTS DEVELOP NORMALLY

Suzanne M. Johnson and Elizabeth O'Connor

The debate over whether children of gay or lesbian parents develop normally has figured prominently in adoption and custody cases involving homosexual parents. In this selection Suzanne M. Johnson and Elizabeth O'Connor summarize research that compares the intellectual functioning, peer relationships, and psychological health of children reared by heterosexual parents and by homosexual parents. They conclude that none of the studies show that children of gay parents mature any differently than other children. Johnson is a professor of psychology and O'Connor is an adjunct faculty member at Dowling College in Long Island, New York.

A question that has been asked, in many different ways, about children being raised by gay men or lesbians is, Are they normal? That is, how do these children compare to their peers who have heterosexual parents? Is their experience so far removed from that of children raised by heterosexual parents that they differ in some fundamental ways from those children? Or, are there subtle distinctions between children of gays and children of heterosexual parents, distinctions that may become evident only once the children reach adulthood?

The adjustment of children raised by gays or lesbians is of more than academic interest. Public discourse, legislation regarding adoptions, and decisions made in courtrooms all rest in part on beliefs about how the children in these families fare. We, then, examine the studies that have looked at this question: Are the children normal?

## Intellectual Functioning

It is not clear what rationale would be used to suggest that children raised by gay or lesbian parents might be lacking in their academic skills, intelligence or general cognitive functioning, and, indeed, none has been advanced. However, some studies of children of gay and lesbian parents have included measures of intellectual functioning. [D.K.]

Flaks, [I.] Ficher, [F.] Masterpasqua, & [G.] Joseph (1995) compared fifteen three- to nine-year-old children born to lesbian couples with fifteen children of the same age born to heterosexual couples. No differences were found on IQ scores between the groups (IQ was assessed either through the Wechsler Intelligence Scale for Children-Revised (WISC-R) or the Wechsler Preschool and Primary Scale of Intelligence, the two most frequently used measures of children's intelligence). Likewise, [R.] Green, [J.B.] Mandel, [M.E.] Hotvedt, [J.] Gray, & [L.] Smith (1986) found no differences on IQ measures between fifty-six children who lived with lesbian mothers and 48 children living with heterosexual mothers, and [M.] Kirkpatrick, [C.] Smith, & [R.] Roy (1981) found no differences in WISC-R IQ scores between children of lesbian mothers and children of heterosexual mothers in their study of twenty children, ages five to twelve, in each group.

## Peer Relationships

Concerns that children with gay or lesbian parents will experience difficulties with their peers, which might range from teasing to harassment to outright ostracism, have been cited by some judges who are reluctant to grant custody to a gay or lesbian parent.

Do children of lesbian and gay parents experience hostility from peers during their early years? When the children in their sample were school age (between five and seventeen years), [S.] Golombok, [S.] Spencer, & [M.] Rutter (1983) collected information about their relationships with other children. (This sample contained thirty-seven children of lesbians and thirty-eight children of heterosexual mothers.) The two groups of children did not differ in the quality of their peer relationships, according to interviews with their mothers. Only two in each group were described as having definite problems with other children. About one-third of the children were described as having some slight difficulties with peers, which included things like being shy or getting into more than the usual number of quarrels.

[R.] Green, [J.B.] Mandel, [M.E.] Hotvedt, [J.] Gray, & [L.] Smith (1986) asked both mothers and their children about their social relationships. Children of lesbian mothers were as likely to rate themselves as popular as were children of heterosexual mothers. The ratings of the lesbian and the heterosexual mothers did not differ, either; they were equally likely to rate their children as sociable and accepted by other children.

These studies were conducted on school-age children. Other studies have focused on adolescence, a period in which developing positive relationships with peers and coping with the need to belong are critically important developmental tasks. Adolescence is thought to be the period when, if ever peer difficulties are going to occur, they will occur. Adolescents are coming to terms with their own sexuality and are thought to be especially sensitive to issues related to sexuality.

[F.L.] Tasker & [S.] Golombok (1997) interviewed the young adults in their sample about their experiences with peers during adolescence. Teasing was a common experience for both groups: more than three-quarters of adolescents in both groups reported having been teased. They found that those with lesbian mothers were no more likely to recall having experienced teasing than were those with heterosexual mothers. Of those in both groups who were teased, there was no difference between the groups in whether they categorized the teasing as serious and prolonged. For young women, there were no differences between the lesbian mother group and the heterosexual mother group in whether they had been teased about their mother's sexuality or about their own. The sons of lesbian mothers were more likely to have been teased about their own sexuality than were the sons of heterosexual mothers. It may be that any association with homosexuality has more negative implications for boys than for girls. For adolescent males, there is a great deal of pressure to be seen as virile and heterosexual. Having a lesbian mother appears to cause other adolescents to question a young man's own sexuality, or at least pretend to question it.

## Psychological Health

The argument that children raised by gay or lesbian parents are likely to develop interpersonal or emotional difficulties is based on two assumptions. The first is that children in these families will experience teasing and ridicule from their peers, which will lead to social isolation and disturbed peer relationships. The second assumption is that the experience of having gay or lesbian parents is in itself so stressful that it will lead to anxiety, depression, or other types of psychological maladjustment.

Researchers have looked at the psychological adjustment of children in gay- and lesbian-headed homes. No differences between children ages three to nine raised in two-parent lesbian homes and children raised in two-parent heterosexual parent homes were found on measures of behavioral-adjustment [according to D.K. Flaks, I. Ficher, F. Masterpasqua, & G. Joseph, 1995]. The children's behavioral adjustment was assessed by each child's biological mother and by each child's teacher, each of whom completed questionnaires that asked about three areas of the child's behavior: internalizing behavior (which includes problems such as depression, anxiety, and fearfulness); externalizing behavior (which includes problems such as aggression, disobedience, and hyperactivity); and social competence (which includes positive behavior such as getting along with peers). In no case was there any significant difference between children of lesbian parents and children of heterosexual parents.

[S.] Golombok, [A.] Spencer, and [M.] Rutter (1983) assessed two groups of children via extensive psychiatric interviews of the children and their mothers. Both groups of children (with rare exception) had been born into a heterosexual relationship and later been through a parental divorce. The mothers of one group of children were now living as lesbians, while the mothers of the other group were living as single heterosexual parents. All of the children now resided with their mothers. The mean age of the children was nine and ten years. No differences between the groups were found in the children's emotional development, behavior, or relationships as assessed by mother or teacher questionnaires. In no case did the children of lesbians fare worse than their counterparts. In fact, according to the maternal interviews, the children of single heterosexual mothers were more likely to have been referred to a psychiatric clinic (although it must be noted that only a small number of them had been referred). Once again, the children in the "lesbian mother group" were living with a parent in a relationship, while the children in the "single heterosexual mother group" were not. This methodological confound is one that appears frequently in studies on lesbian mothers and their children. . . .

A similar study, which examined children living with lesbian and with heterosexual mothers, was undertaken by [M.] Kirkpatrick, [C.] Smith, and [R.] Roy (1981). The children were between the ages of five and twelve, most had been through a parental divorce, and they and their mothers were assessed by a psychologist. The children were also assessed by a psychiatrist. No differences were found between the two groups of children in terms of emotional disturbance or presence of pathology.

## Adolescent Psychological Health

Adolescent children of lesbians have also been studied in terms of their psychological health [T.D.] Gershon, [J.M.] Tschann, and [J.M.] Jemerin (1999) measured the self-esteem of adolescents who were living with their lesbian mothers. Most of the adolescents had been born into heterosexual marriages. Their parents' marriages ended, and their mothers assumed lesbian identities. The results showed that this group's self-esteem scores, including their feelings about their own self-worth, close friendships, and social acceptance, were within the normal range.

Similar findings were reported by [S.L.] Huggins (1989), who found no difference in self-esteem between adolescents with divorced heterosexual mothers and adolescents with divorced lesbian mothers.

Researchers have also examined the possibility that children raised in lesbian or gay households might not exhibit psychological adjustment difficulties until later in life. That is, even if no psychological maladjustment is apparent during childhood, some problems may appear during adulthood. [F.L.] Tasker and [S.] Golombok (1997) examined this question and found no differences in either anxiety or depression (measured by the Trait Anxiety Inventory and the Beck Depression Inventory, respectively) between the two groups of young adults they assessed (one group had been raised by lesbian mothers, the other by divorced heterosexual mothers). The young adults raised by lesbian mothers were no more likely to have sought professional mental health treatment. [J.S.] Gottman (1990) found that adult daughters of lesbians scored within the normal range on measures of social adjustment and did not differ from women who had been raised by either single or remarried divorced mothers.

To summarize, in no study that has looked at the psychological well-being of children raised by lesbian mothers has there been any evidence to suggest that the children are maladjusted. Overall, studies that have assessed children, adolescents, and young adults have found that this group is functioning well.

# SAME-SEX MARRIAGE IS BAD FOR CHILDREN

Dennis Prager

According to Dennis Prager, Americans must oppose same-sex marriage because it is harmful to the natural development of healthy children. He states that the studies that show that children raised by parents of the same sex do just as well as children raised by a mother and a father all contain at least one fatal flaw. Prager argues that men and women contribute distinctive features to parenting and that therefore having a mother and a father is in the best interest of children. Legalizing same-sex marriage would sanction incomplete families and ignore the welfare of children in those families, he says. Dennis Prager is a nationally syndicated radio talk-show host and the author of several books, including *Happiness Is a Serious Problem: A Human Nature Repair Manual* and *Why the Jews? The Reason for Antisemitism.*

Of all the arguments against same-sex marriage, the most immediately compelling is that it hurts children. If children have a right to anything, it is to begin life with a mother and father. Death, divorce, abandonment, a single-parent's mistakes—any one of these deprives children of a mother or father. But only same-sex marriage would legally ensure children are deprived from birth of either a mother or a father.

Why, then, doesn't a child's right to begin life with a mother and father have any impact on the millions of people who either advocate same-sex marriage or can't make up their minds on the issue?

## Ignoring the Welfare of Children

Among gay activists, the reason is narcissism. Though gays already have the right to raise children without an opposite-sex parent, and the right to adopt children, gay activists want society to enshrine one-sex parenting with its highest seal of approval—marriage. For gay activists, the fact that a child does best with a good mother and good father is of no significance (or worse, denied). All that matters is what is good for gays.

And what about the heterosexuals who support same-sex marriage? They ignore the issue of its effects on children because they either do not want to confront the issue or because they are so intimidated by the liberation trinity—"equality," "rights" and "tolerance"—that even children's welfare becomes a non-issue.

Advocates of same-sex marriage have, therefore, many good reasons not to talk about issue of children. Even the most passionate advocate does not argue that it is better for a child to have two mothers and no father or two fathers and no mother.

But, the same-sex marriage advocates will respond, while children may not be better off, they will be just as well off, with two fathers and no mother or two mothers and no father.

This claim, however, is dishonest. So dishonest that it leads to a certain cognitive dissonance among many of those who make it. On the one hand, they don't really believe mothers (or fathers) are useless, and they do not wish to lie. On the other hand, they know they have to say a mother and father are no better for children than two same-sex parents or they will lose the public's support for same-sex marriage.

Were they to admit the obvious truth—that same-sex marriage means society will legally and deliberately deprive increasing numbers of children of either a mother or a father—few Americans would support the legal redefinition of marriage and family.

## False Claims About Children of Gay Parents

So, same-sex marriage advocates now argue that children do not do better with a mother and a father.

To buttress this absurdity, they repeatedly ask, "Where are the studies" that prove children do better with a father and a mother? Not only are there no such studies, they claim, but in fact, "studies show" that children raised with parents of the same sex do just as well as children raised by a father and a mother.

But this claim, too, is dishonest.

As Professor Don Browning of the University of Chicago recently wrote in the *New York Times*, "We know next to nothing" about the effects of same-sex parenting on children."

"The body of sociological knowledge about same-sex parenting," he and his co-author wrote, "is scant at best. . . . There are no rigorous, large-scale studies on the effect of same-sex marriage on the couples' children."

"Steven Nock, a leading scholar of marriage at the University of Virginia, wrote in March 2001 after a thorough review that every study on this question 'contained at least one fatal flaw' and 'not a single one was conducted according to generally accepted standards of scientific research.'"

So the statement that "studies show" that children don't do better with a mother and father is as factually mendacious as it is morally repugnant. Why then are so many fooled by it? *Because "studies show" has become the refuge of those who do not wish to think.* I hear this lack of thought regularly from college-educated callers to my radio show who refuse to think an issue through, or to make a moral judgment, without first having seen what "studies show."

## The Bottom Line

But does anyone who thinks, rather than awaits "studies" to affirm their biases, really believe a mother is useless if a child has two fathers, or a father is unnecessary if a child has two mothers? The idea that men and women do not have entirely distinctive contributions to make to the rearing of a child is so absurd that it is frightening that many well-educated—and only the well-educated—people believe it.

There are many powerful arguments against same-sex marriage. . . . But if you have to offer only one, know that those who push for same-sex marriage base their case on something factually indefensible—that children do not benefit from having a father and a mother; and on something morally indefensible—ignoring what is best for children.

# THE *WILL & GRACE* EFFECT

Debra Rosenberg

Whether a person supports the legalization of gay marriage may have a lot to do with his or her age, according to Debra Rosenberg. Writing on the eve of the legalization of gay marriage in Massachusetts, Rosenberg reports that recent opinion polls have shown that younger generations are much more likely to look favorably on same-sex marriage than older ones. Many eighteen- to twenty-nine-year-olds see legalizing gay marriage as a way to assimilate gays and lesbians into the mainstream society. Others view gay marriage as a necessary civil rights advancement rather than as a religious issue. Older generations have a stronger tendency to believe same-sex marriage is antiestablishment, unnatural, or immoral. The difference in opinion likely results from the higher rate of exposure of younger generations to gay and lesbian issues in the media and popular culture. TV shows such as *Will & Grace*, whose lead male character is gay, are contributing to greater acceptance of homosexuality in these younger generations. Debra Rosenberg is a writer for *Newsweek* magazine.

For Richard and Jeanine Benanti, opposing same-sex marriage was an easy call. "It's against nature, it's against society and it's against the Bible," says 49-year-old Richard, who works for the Boys and Girls Club in Springfield, Ill. His wife, Jeanine, a 46-year-old stay-at-home mom, shared his feelings. "The way I was raised, as a Catholic, marriage was always between one man and one woman," she says. "I don't see how you could make it anything else." The Benantis took their three children to church regularly and sent them to Catholic school. So it was a shock when their 18-year-old daughter, Diana, recently announced her support for gay marriage. Diana says her views solidified after she saw a just-married gay couple on TV. "I just thought how sweet it was that they finally got what they wanted," she says. "Allowing them to be married is something that America is all about."

Maybe not all of America—yet. Thousands of gay couples tied the knot in a few rogue counties in California, Oregon and other states, but court battles stopped the flow of licenses, some of which were legally questionable to begin with. This week [of May 24, 2004], after years of legal wrangling, Massachusetts becomes the first state to allow same-sex unions with the blessing of its highest court. This time, brides and grooms won't be forced to rush through assembly-line weddings at city hall, but are heading to reception halls, sympathetic churches and picturesque beaches for ceremonies with all the customary frills. That's given a new urgency to the arguments on both sides in the marriage debate. Opponents believe the images of more gay newlyweds will so offend the public that conservatives will win new support for their continuing efforts to ban same-sex unions. Late last week [of May 17, 2004] they tried, and failed, to get the U.S. Supreme Court to issue an emergency stay. But supporters say the Massachusetts weddings will prove gay marriage isn't a threat to anyone. "Gays are not going to use up all the marriage licenses," says Evan Wolfson, director of Freedom to Marry.

The debate isn't just dividing Americans by state—in many families it's the cause of friction at the dinner table. Polls show a sizeable generation gap when it comes to supporting same-sex marriage. In a NEWSWEEK Poll, 41 percent of 18- to 29-year-olds back gay marriage, compared with 28 percent of Americans overall. Generation Y is more tolerant than its elders, says pollster Celinda Lake. Christine Dinnino, 17, has regular fights about the marriage issue with her father, Samuel, a 43-year-old retired Army sergeant in Inverness, Fla. Though Samuel bases his objections on the Bible, Christine sees gay marriage as a civil-rights issue. "It used to be illegal to marry someone of a different race," she says. "That sounds pretty foreign to the typical 15-year-old today." While baby boomers tend to view homosexuality as anti-establishment, young people often see same-sex marriage as a way of integrating gays into society, says demographer Neil Howe, who has written about differences among the generations. "They see it," he says, "as domesticating something that might be threatening to society and making it mainstream."

Younger people may also be more accepting because they've had greater exposure to gay people than previous generations had. Fewer gays are closeted, and the average age for "coming out" is now 16, down from the mid-20s in the 1970s. Knowing someone who is openly gay or lesbian is the single biggest predictor of tolerance on same-sex marriage, says Wolfson. And if you don't personally know someone who's gay, you'll find plenty of gay characters and culture on TV. Recent research by Edward Schiappa, a professor of communications at the University of Minnesota, found that seeing likable gay characters on shows like "Will & Grace" had similar effects to knowing gays in real life. In one study, students with few or no gay acquaintances were shown 10 episodes of HBO's "Six Feet Under." Afterward, their levels of anti-gay prejudice dropped by 12 percent.

Cultural conservatives are all too aware that such sympathetic portrayals of gay life can only hurt their efforts to portray same-sex marriage as a threat to American culture. "This generation has been subjected to an enormous amount of pro-gay propaganda," says Robert Knight, director of the Culture and Family Institute at Concerned Women for America.

Even so, there wasn't much opponents could do to stop this week's weddings. Gov. Mitt Romney—a Republican who leans conservative on social issues, even in this most Democratic of states—fought the November court decision approving same-sex marriages. He then pushed for a constitutional amendment to ban them. One version passed the state legislature but must be ratified again by lawmakers and voters—and wouldn't take effect before 2006. In the meantime, eager to preserve his national prospects within the GOP, Romney tried to bar out-of-state couples from tying the knot. Marriage opponents still complained that Romney didn't go far enough. Last week former GOP presidential candidate Alan Keyes launched a $40,000 TV and radio ad campaign chiding Romney for refusing to help recall the four state supreme court judges who backed gay marriage. A weary Romney seemed resigned to the inevitable last week: he said he would attend gay weddings if invited.

Massachusetts may be the first state to open its doors to gays, but it likely won't be the last. The National Gay and Lesbian Task Force estimates that pro-marriage lawsuits are underway in 10 states. And though only local couples are supposed to marry in Massachusetts, some out-of-staters could get hitched and then demand legal rights back home. More than a dozen states are trying to head off those maneuvers with anti-gay-marriage measures on the ballot this fall. With both sides so entrenched, "it's very difficult to change minds on this," says pollster Robert Meadow. If present trends hold, Meadow says, gay-marriage opponents will eventually find themselves outnumbered—in the courts, in statehouses and around the dinner table.

CHAPTER 3

# LEGAL AND POLICY ISSUES CONFRONTING GAYS AND LESBIANS

Contemporary Issues
Companion

# GAYS AND LESBIANS ARE GAINING POLITICAL POWER

Diana Ray

In recent times politically active gays and lesbians have tended to wield power as a sophisticated interest group working within the political establishment rather than through the militant gay movement of previous decades. In this selection Diana Ray reports that in the 1990s, an unprecedented number of gays and lesbians gained political ground by becoming involved in both the Republican and Democratic parties. The change was largely due to the 1992 Clinton presidential campaigns, active solicitation of the gay vote, and attention to the issue of gays in the military. In the new millennium, gays and lesbians are packing political conventions, running for office, and operating influential political organizations. Two examples of their mass mobilization include the boycott of the *Dr. Laura Schlessinger Show* on television (due to her assertion that homosexuality is abnormal) and the battle to allow gay troop leaders in the Boy Scouts of America. In these campaigns and many others, the Internet has become an essential tool for organizing and informing gay and lesbian voters and activists. Ray is a reporter for *Insight on the News*.

Gays and lesbians continue to gain ground politically and are seeking greater acceptance and influence in both the Democratic and Republican parties.

Ron Smith is openly gay, divorced and the father of a 7-year-old boy who doesn't know his father is a homosexual. Although he is a civilian now, Smith served as an open gay in the U.S. Army during the Clinton administration. His friends and family are straight. His roommate is straight. And when asked about his gay activism, he is thrilled. "I am so glad you asked. I never get to talk about it," he tells *Insight*.

But Smith is one of the angry activists who have gained momentum on high-profile issues such as Paramount's decision to support the *Dr. Laura Schlessinger Show* on TV because of the hostess' opposition to homosexual conduct. Smith never had listened to Dr. Laura, a straight arrow if ever there was one, but when the call to arms came through gay Websites to attack the TV program, Smith responded and contacted its commercial sponsors through gay-community e-mail and with signed petitions.

## The New Gay Activism

Whether the issue is Dr. Laura, the Boy Scouts, military service or getting more openly gay candidates into positions of power, gay activism is here, persistent, but no longer self-consciously offensive.

In fact, it has come a long way since the 1969 Stonewall tavern riot in New York City that first mobilized homosexuals and initiated a militant gay movement that sometimes has sought to assault and insult the institutions of traditional morality in the name of equality.

"Gays and lesbians are emerging as a distinctive interest group," says Steve Sanders, who for four years has been teaching a class on gay politics at Indiana University. "They have moved from being a social movement to more of an interest group with established lobbying groups, political-action committees and a distinctive voting profile. It's a group that is out and is exercising influence." Assistant to the dean of the College of Arts and Sciences and openly homosexual, Sanders proposed to teach the class because of his own involvement in gay politics and because he felt there was an interest on campus.

University classes such as the one Sanders teaches are not new. Sixty-year-old political-science professor Ron Hunt has been teaching classes on gay politics at Ohio University in Athens for 20 years. Hunt, who also is openly gay, says, "I started teaching the class when I first came to Ohio. I had slowly and surely come out as an openly gay professor and, in the late 1970s, was approached by grad students to do an independent course on gay politics. After a time it dawned on me that I had enough material to teach regularly scheduled classes on the subject. I taught it as an experimental course for two years and, afterward, got it approved through the curriculum."

Now, Hunt says, he keeps the class size to about 50, but interest has grown to the extent that the course always closes because it fills up.

Hunt and Sanders agree that the gay movement gained great momentum with Bill Clinton in 1992 when he was the first presidential candidate to address gays at fund-raisers and include them in his vision for America. "Clinton was the first to acknowledge and ask for the gay vote, and he established a gay and lesbian liaison officer within the White House," says Sanders. That, coupled with the inclusion of gay identification in exit polls for the first time in the 1990s, and the issue of gays in the military raised early in the Clinton administration, helped to solidify the community's identity as a valid interest group.

"It is no longer a phenomenon of radical activists screaming in the streets, but one of having money, influence and working for influence," Sanders tells *Insight.*

## Gay Interest Groups

But the movement is hard to define in numbers, since there are no definitive studies on what percentage of the population is gay, according to the Gay and Lesbian Task Force in Washington. Estimates range between 1 and 3 percent, although some questionable studies claim the figure could be as high as 10 percent. Usually, however, activists include family members and friends of gays who may be straight and often don't agree with the mainstream gay community.

While serving under Clinton's "don't ask, don't tell" policy, Ron Smith became convinced that homosexuals can serve harmoniously within the military and should be allowed to do so. "Every one should have a shot, if they want to," he says. But as far as the Boy Scouts go, Smith says he sees no problem with the Supreme Court decision this year allowing the Scouts to ban homosexual leaders. "I was a Boy Scout growing up and I think the Scouts should be allowed to do what they want in peace. The gay community should respect their beliefs and right to do so."

Although Smith's perspective does not parallel that of prominent gay political organizations, it is people like him who are turning to those groups to stay informed and have influence, says Sloan Wiesen of the Gay and Lesbian Victory Fund. The fund is a national organization with the sole mission of increasing the number of openly gay and lesbian political candidates. According to Wiesen, it was founded in 1991 and has helped nearly to quadruple openly gay officials from 49 to 200 across the country. "In most of America . . . our community remains largely without representation in our government, and we have found that we can help fix the discrimination problems by addressing the representation problem."

Wiesen says his organization has contributed $2.5 million to candidates during the last decade. Before the November [2000] elections, there were three openly gay representatives in the Congress: Barney Frank, D-Mass., Jim Kolbe, R-Ariz. and Tammie Baldwin, D-Wis. Additionally, [2000] saw the first openly gay U.S. Senate nominee of a major party, Democrat Ed Flanagan of Vermont.

## Democrats vs. Republicans

Sloan calls it progress that [the 2000 election was] the first presidential election in which the support of the gay community has been solicited openly by candidates as early as the primaries. He says that so far the Democratic Party is seen by gays as the more sympathetic.

In a 1996 article for the *Harvard Gay & Lesbian Review*, Barney Frank wrote: "At every level of government, and in every region of the country, the Democrats are significantly better than the Republicans on the issue of defeating homophobia and protecting us against unfair discrimination. Why, then, the ambivalence on the part of gay men and lesbians about following the advice of Samuel Gompers, who in the early days of the labor movement in America announced the political principle that he said should govern those seeking to use the political process to advance important goals: reward your friends and punish your enemies? For gays and lesbians in the current American political climate, this means strongly supporting Democrats nearly all the time."

The number of openly gay delegates at [the 2000] Democratic National Convention was nearly double that of 1996, says the Democratic National Committee, and the party has its own gay and lesbian outreach coordinator. The Republican National Committee tells *Insight* it refers all outreach inquiries to the Log Cabin Republicans (LCR), an independent gay organization. But Kevin Ivers of the LCR says the real political debates on gay issues concerning discrimination are happening within the Republican Party because the Democrats have taken the community for granted. He says that although the Democrats have organized outreach groups, those entities do not have autonomy and must carry the complete line of the Democratic Party to get support. Ivers claims that exit polls show 25 to 33 percent of voters claiming to be gay say they vote Republican.

Both Democratic and GOP political activists tell *Insight* that their goal of acceptance never will happen until both parties embrace the gay community as equals within the political culture. The professors and other activists point to the increasing number of gay characters on television and increasing news coverage of gay issues as having helped to integrate the community's acceptance into the mainstream culture while giving young people gay and lesbian role models.

## Internet Activism

Besides more entertainment celebrities and elected officials, the last two years have seen a revolution in communication within the gay community with the aid of the Internet. It offers gays the opportunity to be both discreet and involved, as well as providing a vast amount of news and information pertaining to gays. America Online's gay Website, Planet Out, informs visitors that "The 2000 presidential election is a crucial one for gay men and lesbians. It will go a long way toward determining whether the progress of the last decade continues or the clock is turned back on gay rights." Planet Out and other sites effectively keep readers in tune with related political and social issues and offer ways to get involved, such as joining gay political organizations like the Human Rights Campaign (HRC), whose annual budget now is $20 million and membership 250,000, according to HRC spokesman Wayne Besen.

"With the Internet," Besen says, "gays can come out at their own pace. It has been huge for young men and women or those that are isolated." The downside, he says, is that it has attracted hate groups.

Smith originally learned of the Dr. Laura issue on the nightly news but, within 24 hours, he tells *Insight*, he was receiving and responding to action-alert mailings through organizations such as HRC. One of the most visible was the StopDrLaura.com Website created over a four-day period by 36-year-old John Avaroses of Washington with the help of a few friends. Avaroses writes a mailer called "The List" that discusses gay issues and had included comments on the Dr. Laura issue. He says the response was so overwhelming that he decided to write an action alert that read, in part:

"When *60 Minutes'* Andy Rooney belittled Native Americans, he got suspended. . . . When Jimmy the Greek stereotyped blacks, he got fired. . . . But when Dr. Laura calls gays biological mistakes, she gets a TV show from Paramount. Enough is enough."

The alert elicited so much response that Avaroses and his friends decided to create their Website to keep the public informed on the issue. "This whole campaign has been running on $15,000, a majority of which was raised selling T-shirts on our Website. It has grown into a movement, and everyone is welcome," Avaroses tells *Insight*. He says about 20 percent of the funding came from private individual donations and from the Gay & Lesbian Alliance Against Defamation.

How long will the campaign continue? "Until the show is cancelled," says Avaroses. The Website includes daily updates of who is advertising and who is not, as well as excerpts from advertiser explanations for reconsidering sponsorship of the program.[1]

"It's impossible to overestimate how important e-mail has been to linking people," says gay-politics instructor Sanders. "Just a couple of major Websites, including StopDrLaura.com, have allowed lots of people to monitor the *Dr. Laura Show* on a daily basis saying, 'Here are the advertisers and here's how you can e-mail consumer affairs to let them know how you object.'"

Besen from the HRC agrees: "With the Internet, it's easier for gays and lesbians to become more active and get connected: People are coming out sooner and realizing injustices."

## Mobilizing Against the Boy Scouts of America

One of those injustices, according to Besen, is the Supreme Court decision to allow the Boy Scouts to ban homosexuals from participation as Scout leaders. Although Besen acknowledges the Boy Scouts as a fine institution, he uses an analogy comparing the group to the Ku Klux Klan.

1. The Dr. Laura Schlessinger television show premiered in September 2000. Many of the show's advertisers pulled their support due to her controversial remarks about gays and lesbians. The show was cancelled in late March 2001, after reaching a low nationwide Nielsen rating of 132.

"Any analogy, of Boy Scouts to the Ku Klux Klan is offensive," says Gregg Shields, a spokesman for the Boy Scouts. "The Boy Scouts of America does not preach hate. It preaches respect and kindness toward all. In terms of access to schools, we ask to be treated as any other not-for-profit organization under the school's policy."

Since the Supreme Court decision, numerous school boards, city councils and charities such as the United Way have been persuaded by gay activists to halt or reduce support. But Shields isn't concerned. "If we were to take a major hit tomorrow, tomorrow night the planned Boy Scout meetings will still go on," he tells *Insight*. "If we received a huge donation of money tomorrow, but we didn't have Scouts coming to the meetings, Scouting wouldn't happen. That's what's critical."

United Way spokesman Phil Jones says the United Way does not dictate to local chapters concerning their funding, but he tells *Insight* that only 20 or so chapters out of 1,400 have reconsidered funding for the Boy Scouts. Of those that have reconsidered, only a few have stopped funding the Boy Scouts completely. "Supporters of the Boy Scouts have been very vocal at the national level, but I have to keep telling people that the decision to affect Boy Scout funding is at the local level, and that it is those chapters that must be contacted."

Shields says, "We've been litigating this for 20 years. Girls have sued to be Boy Scouts, atheists and agnostics have wanted to be leaders and they have all lost." Shields notes the organization was sued unsuccessfully in 1980 by a homosexual adult who wanted to participate openly. In the same year, when a 19-year-old scoutmaster assistant in New Jersey joined a university gay and lesbian association, he was asked to end his relationship with the Boy Scouts. He also sued, but lost in the lower court, and that is the case that made it to the Supreme Court in 2000.

According to Sanders, the Supreme Court decision probably has helped the gay movement. "I think it's been a good thing because it has led to such tremendous organized efforts among the gay community."

But as vocal as organized gays have been on the issue, Shields denies that he's worried. "We can certainly have tolerance and respect and we don't have to accept everyone's belief and don't have to accept everyone. We're not a fund-driven organization. We are a mission-driven organization. And our supporters have made it clear they want this organization and the principles it teaches."

# HATE CRIMES LEGISLATION AND HOMOSEXUALITY

Gordon A. Babst

Hate crimes legislation is designed to increase penalties for convicted perpetrators whose crimes are motivated by bias toward a group of people such as gays and lesbians. Many Americans support hate crimes legislation protecting racial and religious groups but reject legislation that would include sexual orientation and gender identity as additional protected categories. In the following selection Gordon A. Babst examines the controversy over expanding the scope of hate crimes laws to include sexual orientation and gender identity. He surveys the problem of violence against gays, lesbians, and transgendered people; reviews the history of federal hate crimes legislation; and considers arguments for and against increasing penalties for hate crimes. Babst is a professor of political science at Chapman University in California and the author of *Liberal Constitutionalism, Marriage, and Sexual Orientation: A Contemporary Case for Dis-Establishment.*

Hate Crimes is a recent category in the law that distinguishes crimes against a person or his or her property when motivated by bias towards a group of groups from the same crimes when not animated by the offending bias. Types of offending bias include crimes motivated by the victim's race, color, religion, national origin, and, more controversially, sexual orientation and gender identity.

Whereas demarcating a category in the law for crimes animated by a desire to inflict some form of harm on a member of a group characterized by its racial heritage or religious beliefs may rest comfortably with most Americans, who tend to react negatively against racial or religious bias, the inclusion of sexual orientation and gender identity as categories has proved more challenging, perhaps because of the ambiguous social status of gay men, lesbians, and transgendered persons in American society, or in the case of gender, the question of whether it is appropriate to consider crimes of rape or domestic violence, already fairly well-delineated in the criminal law, as hate crimes against women.

Although the categories sexual orientation and gender identity do not specify which orientations or identities are protected (and indeed all orientations and identities are covered when such categories are included in hate crimes legislation), it is often assumed that such categories convey some kind of "special" rights on homosexual or transgendered persons.

The challenge has been to persuade Americans that crimes against gay men, lesbians, or transgendered people, when motivated by animus towards all homosexuals or towards homosexuality in general, or toward all transgendered people, merit condemnation, just as do crimes motivated by racial or religious animus.

## Violence Against Gays, Lesbians, and Transgendered People

The problem of violence directed against gay men and lesbians and those who do not conform to gender expectations is a serious one. Gay bashing is pervasive in many areas of the world and in the lives of most glbtq [gay, lesbian, bisexual, transgendered, and queer] people.

The National Gay and Lesbian Task Force released a report in 1984 that documented the extent of violence directed against glbtq people in the United States. Based on a survey of nearly 2,000 gay men and lesbians in eight cities, the report indicated that almost all of the respondents had experienced some form of verbal, physical, or property-related abuse.

Gay men, lesbians, and transgendered people are less likely to report abuse than other groups, largely because of fear of police brutality or public exposure. Some sources indicate that as much as 90 percent of all antigay crimes goes unreported.

In response to the problem of violence directed toward members of the glbtq community, many organizations, usually in larger cities, have formed antiviolence task forces and patrols, aimed to creating safe spaces for members of the community, opening dialogue with police authorities, and gathering statistics regarding the prevalence of hate crimes in the glbtq community. Others have monitored courtrooms to make certain that individuals charged with hate crimes are prosecuted fully. Still others have campaigned for hate crimes legislation.

Although the move for hate crimes legislation began in the mid-1980s, some particularly graphic examples of hate crimes against glbtq people in the 1990s gave urgency to the movement, especially the gruesome murders of lesbian crossdresser Brandon Teena in 1993 (the subject of Susan Muska and Greta Olafsdottir's documentary *The Brandon Teena Story* [1997] and Kimberly Peirce's feature *Boys Don't Cry* [1999]), Wyoming college student Matthew Shepard in 1998, and Alabama textile worker Billy Jack Gaither in 1999.

Although these brutal murders were all too familiar to glbtq people, they garnered a great deal of media attention. They thereby made the problem of antigay violence real for the larger public.

[As of 2004] 29 states and the District of Columbia have hate crimes statutes that include sexual orientation. Eight states also include gender identity protection, while another 17 states have hate crimes statutes that do not include either sexual orientation or gender identity. Four states have no hate crimes legislation whatsoever.

## Federal Hate Crimes Legislation

Perhaps the most important development in hate crimes law is the adoption of federal hate crimes legislation.

The *Hate Crimes Statistics Act* took effect in 1990, having been signed into law by President George Bush at a public ceremony in the Rose Garden of the White House, the first ceremony there officially to include members of the gay and lesbian community.

This law asks local law enforcement officials, on a voluntary basis, to gather and maintain statistics on the incidence of hate crimes, including those motivated by bias on the basis of sexual orientation, so as to ascertain the extent of the problem and whether to legislate further hate crimes laws. In 2001 there were 9,730 hate crimes reported by the F.B.I. in its Uniform Crime Report, about 14% of which based on sexual orientation.

The *Hate Crimes Sentencing Enhancement Act* took effect in 1994, and provides for perhaps the most controversial aspect of any hate crimes legislation, an enhanced penalty for convicted perpetrators of hate crimes, but it did not cover sexual orientation, gender, or disability as categories to be protected.

In 2000, a bill introduced into the Senate as the *Hate Crimes Prevention Act* was revised and renamed the *Local Law Enforcement Enhancement Act* [LLEEA] by the House of Representatives. This bill, were it passed, would add sexual orientation, gender, and disability to the categories, and bring some uniformity to the nation's hate crimes laws. It would mandate federal prosecution should the hate crimes have been violent, or occurred on federal lands, or hindered a person in the exercise of a civil right. This bill has not been passed into law, but it continues to be introduced each congressional term.

## Critiques of Enhanced Penalties

Critics of hate crimes legislation have charged that such legislation in effect makes certain groups of Americans more worthy, and other groups less worthy, because the "same" crime committed against a group not enumerated in hate crimes legislation does not merit as severe a punishment as when committed against a member of a protected group.

Some critics have further argued that enhanced sentencing punishes thought because the only differences between an ordinary crime and the "same" crime when motivated by bias is the animating bias, and all Americans, even criminals, have freedom of expression and should not be punished for their thoughts.

## The Argument for Enhanced Sentencing

A defender of hate crimes legislation might reply that a crime motivated by hate is not the "same" crime at all, but a different one, warranting a different response from the criminal justice system, including the possibility of a stiffer sentence. Were the animating motive absent, the crime would not have occurred. Moreover, the criminal law routinely considers motive, as in making distinctions between murder in the first degree, homicide, and manslaughter, even though the victim is as dead in each case.

Perhaps the best argument in favor of hate crime legislation is that such crimes are attacks not merely against an individual, but also against the entire group of which he or she is, or is perceived to be, a member. They are "message crimes," usually addressed to groups that are particularly vulnerable.

Consequently, hate crimes intimidate, degrade, and affect psychologically not merely the individual attacked, but all members of the associated group. They tear at the fabric of American society by reinforcing negative stereotypes about certain groups, and imply that some groups are legitimate targets.

Laws against hate crimes are based on the assumption that all Americans are equal and deserve equal protection. Ignoring hate crimes in the law gives the impression that the state is unmoved when groups of Americans are singled out because of a social bias against them.

In addition, having statutes against hate crimes makes it far less easy for members of the criminal justice system, including police, prosecutors, judges, and juries, to discriminate against victims of hate crimes. With the enactment of hate crimes laws, these officials are less likely to fail to take the victim seriously or to multiply the victim's injury by not investigating the crime or prosecuting the perpetrators to the fullest extent of the law simply because they share in the social prejudice against the victim's group.

## Bias Crime Indicators

To determined whether a hate crime has occurred, trained law enforcement officials review factors known as "bias crime indicators," such as racial, ethnic, or cultural differences, comments or written statements, gestures or graffiti, membership in organized hate groups, and lack of other motives.

These factors suggest that the crime was not random, and that the victim was specifically targeted *because* of her or his race, religion, or sexual orientation, for example. Although a victim may allege a hate crime has occurred, or a prosecutor may pursue a conviction for an alleged hate crime, this is by no means a guarantee that a judge or jury will be persuaded that what occurred was not simply an ordinary crime.

Between 1991 and 2000, for example, the Department of Justice pursued only 37 prosecutions under a hate crimes law because, among other reasons, in the thousands of other cases the evidence warranting the upward adjustment of the category of crime and penalty was deemed insufficient, and lesser crime and penalty were more likely to be prosecuted successfully.

## Hate Crimes Against Gay Men and Lesbians

Hate crimes based on sexual orientation are not the most frequently reported type of hate crime. Such crimes constitute about 14% of all reported hate crimes by category. However, when these crimes are violent, they tend to be particularly brutal, involving, for example, pummeling with a baseball bat, or multiple gunshot wounds, or stabbing.

Such violence may indicated that the perpetrator intends thoroughly to wipe out his victim, having targeted the gay man or lesbian for just this purpose, and for no other, and may suggest that the gay and lesbian community itself is slated for eradication.

# THE MILITARY POLICY TOWARD HOMOSEXUALS

Gregory Herek

In this selection Gregory Herek provides the historical context of the U.S. military's policies against homosexuality. He describes the history of the integration of African American soldiers in the military and contrasts it with the history of gays and lesbians in the military. Unlike racial integration, which eventually won widespread support in the armed forces, acceptance of homosexual soldiers has not increased over the years. Before World War II the military did not officially exclude or discharge homosexuals from its ranks. Instead, it only purged those people suspected of actually engaging in homosexual acts. In 1942, however, the military changed its regulations to prevent gays and lesbians from serving at all. In 1993 the Department of Defense implemented its "Don't Ask, Don't Tell, Don't Pursue" policy that prevented military personnel from being asked about their sexual orientation; however, anyone who had sexual relations with someone of the same sex could still be discharged. The controversial policy remains in force today, fueling a debate about whether gays and lesbians should serve in the armed forces. Herek is a professor of psychology at the University of California, Davis, and has published numerous books and articles about homophobia, hate crimes, and the AIDS stigma. His most recent books are *Stigma and Sexual Orientation: Understanding Prejudice Against Lesbians, Gay Men, and Bisexuals* and *AIDS and Stigma in the United States*.

The military's current policy can be better understood in historical context. A historical perspective is also relevant to comparing policies toward service by gay and lesbian personnel and policies affecting racial minorities, mainly African Americans.

Since the birth of the Republic, government decisions have been made about who shall be permitted or required to serve in the U.S.

Gregory Herek, "Lesbians and Gay Men in the U.S. Military: Historical Background," *Sexual Orientation: Science, Education, and Policy*. http://psychology.ucdavis.edu, 2000.

military, and under what conditions. These decisions have frequently reflected society's attitudes toward its stigmatized minorities. Early in the Revolutionary war, for example, Black Americans were barred from service in the Continental Army. Similarly, Negroes were barred from military service early in the Civil War, despite the eagerness of many Northern Blacks to volunteer. Both policies were later reversed—when, respectively, the British began offering freedom to Black slaves who would join their side, and the Union Army faced a serious shortage of troops.

When they were allowed to serve, Black soldiers were treated differently from their White counterparts. Although led by White officers, they were segregated from White troops. When not in battle, they were often assigned to menial occupations in peripheral units. After the Civil War, for example, Blacks were assigned to distant outposts where they fought against Indians. Dining World War I, most African-Americans were assigned noncombat duties and menial jobs, such as mess orderlies. All-Black units were commanded by White officers, who typically considered such an assignment to be stigmatizing.

At the beginning of World War II, as in the past, personnel needs dictated that Black recruits be accepted for military service. Once again, Black enlisted personnel were segregated from Whites—usually led by Black officers—and placed in support roles. As the war effort progressed, however, the Navy experimented with integration of enlisted personnel, which was less expensive than maintaining combat-ready segregated units.

By the War's end, more than one million African-Americans served efficiently in various service branches. Inter-racial conflict did not appear to be a problem in combat zones, although some tensions were reported in rear areas. As [S.A.] Stouffer and his colleagues concluded in their social scientific study of the American soldier, events in World War II demonstrated that Blacks were effective fighters and that racial integration in the military would not compromise unit effectiveness.

## Ending Racial Segregation and Discrimination

Nevertheless, racial segregation remained official government policy until President Harry Truman's historic Executive Order 9981, issued a few months before the 1948 election, which "declared to be the policy of the President that there shall be equality of treatment and opportunity for all persons in the armed services without regard to race, color, religion, or national origin." Following this order, the armed forces began slowly to institute a policy of racial desegregation. Desegregation proceeded slowly, however, and met with resistance.

As in past wars, the Korean conflict created a shortage of personnel and Black Americans helped to fill this need. Because of troop shortages and the high costs of maintaining racially segregated facilities, integration rapidly became a reality. In 1951, integration of the Army was boosted by the findings from a study of the impact of desegregation on unit effectiveness of troops deployed in Korea. The researchers concluded that racial integration had not impaired task performance or unit effectiveness, that cooperation in integrated units was equal or superior to that of all-White units, and that serving with Blacks appeared to make White soldiers more accepting of integration. By the end of the Korean conflict, the Department of Defense (DOD) had eliminated all racially segregated units and living quarters.

By the 1960s, the proportion of Black personnel had dramatically increased. Evidence remained, however, of both personal and institutional discrimination. At this time, the DOD took new and stronger steps to combat racial discrimination, including housing and other types of discrimination in civilian areas near military installations. The DOD also established civil rights offices to monitor the treatment of minorities. Because of lack of personnel and resources, however, these offices were only minimally effective.

In the late 1960s, racial tensions resulted in violent confrontations between Blacks and Whites, significantly affecting morale. As a consequence, the service branches instituted a variety of programs designed to address racial inequities and reduce interracial conflict. In 1971, the Secretary of Defense established the Defense Race Relations Institute (DRRI), which was later renamed the Defense Equal Opportunity Management Institute (DEOMI).

DRRI/DEOMI has developed and implemented a series of race relations and equal opportunity training programs with an evolving scope. Early efforts, for example, included extensive coverage of racial and ethnic minority history, as well as sensitivity training to the perspectives of minority personnel. Later programs focused less on attitude change and sensitivity training, and more on behavioral compliance with nondiscrimination policies and regulations. From 1971 to late 1992, DEOMI trained 12,352 recruits in race relations and equal opportunity issues.

## Homosexuals and the Military

In contrast to its escalating efforts to promote racial integration and its increasingly nonrestrictive policies concerning gender, opposition in the armed forces to admitting and retaining gay male and lesbian members has intensified since World War II. Historically, the military did not officially exclude or discharge homosexuals from its ranks, although sodomy (usually defined as anal and sometimes oral sex between men) was considered a criminal offense as early as Revolutionary War times. Throughout U.S. history, campaigns have purged military units of persons suspected of engaging in homosexual acts.

As the United States prepared for World War II, psychiatric screening became a part of the induction process and psychiatry's view of homosexuality as an indicator of psychopathology was introduced into the military. Instead of retaining its previous focus on homosexual *behavior*, which was classified as a criminal offense, the military shifted to eliminating homosexual *persons*, based on a medical rationale. In 1942, revised army mobilization regulations included for the first time a paragraph defining both the homosexual and "normal" person and clarifying procedures for rejecting gay draftees.

Homosexual Americans were allowed to serve, however, when personnel shortages necessitated it. As expansion of the war effort required that all available personnel be utilized, screening procedures were loosened and many homosexual men and women enlisted and served. This shift was temporary. As the need for recruits diminished near the war's end, antihomosexual policies were enforced with increasing vigilance, and many gay men and lesbians were discharged involuntarily. Throughout the 1950s and 1960s, acknowledging a homosexual orientation barred an individual from military service.

## Struggles for Gay Rights

In the 1970s, however, a new movement emerged in the United States that pressed for civil rights for gay men and lesbians. The military policy was one target of this movement, dramatized by the legal challenge to the policy mounted by Leonard Matlovich [a gay sergeant who successfully contested his discharge from the air force for being homosexual]. Similar challenges continued throughout the 1970s. Although largely unsuccessful, they highlighted the wide latitude of discretion allowed to commanders in implementing existing policy, which resulted in considerable variation in the rigor with which the policy was enforced.

In 1981, the DOD formulated a new policy which stated unequivocally that homosexuality is incompatible with military service (DOD Directive 1332.14, January 28, 1982, Part 1, Section H). According to a 1992 report by the Government Accounting Office (GAO), nearly 17,000 men and women were discharged under the category of homosexuality in the 1980s. The Navy was disproportionately represented, accounting for 51% of the discharges even though it comprised only 27% of the active force during this time period. Statistical breakdowns by gender and race revealed that, for all services, White women were discharged at a rate disproportionate to their representation. Overall, White females represented 6.4% of personnel but 20.2% of those discharged for homosexuality.

By the end of the 1980s, reversing the military's policy was emerging as a priority for advocates of gay and lesbian civil rights. Several lesbian and gay male members of the armed services came out publicly and vigorously challenged their discharges through the legal system. In 1992, legislation to overturn the ban was introduced in the U.S. Congress. By that time, grassroots civilian opposition to the DOD's policy appeared to be increasing. Many national organizations had officially condemned the policy and many colleges and universities had banned military recruiters and Reserve Officers Training Corps (ROTC) programs from their campuses in protest of the policy.

## "Don't Ask, Don't Tell, Don't Pursue"

By the beginning of 1993, it appeared that the military's ban on gay personnel would soon be overturned. Shortly after his inauguration, President Clinton asked the Secretary of Defense to prepare a draft policy to end discrimination on the basis of sexual orientation, and he proposed to use the interim period to resolve "the real, practical problems that would be involved" in implementing a new policy. Clinton's proposal, however, was greeted with intense opposition from the Joint Chiefs of Staff, members of Congress, the political opposition, and a considerable segment of the U.S. public.

After lengthy public debate and congressional hearings, the President and Senator Sam Nunn (D-GA), chair of the Senate Armed Services Committee, reached a compromise which they labeled "Don't Ask, Don't Tell, Don't Pursue." Under its terms, military personnel would not be asked about their sexual orientation and would not be discharged simply for being gay. Engaging in sexual conduct with a member of the same sex, however, would still constitute grounds for discharge. In the fall of 1993, the congress voted to codify most aspects of the ban. Meanwhile, the civilian courts issued contradictory opinions, with some upholding the policy's constitutionality and others ordering the reinstatement of openly gay military personnel who were involuntarily discharged. Higher courts, however, consistently upheld the policy, making review of the policy by the U.S. Supreme Court unlikely.

The policy has remained in effect since 1993, although the Servicemembers Legal Defense Network and other organizations monitoring its implementation have repeatedly pointed out its failures. Discharges have actually increased under the policy, and harassment of gay and lesbian personnel appears to have intensified in many locales.

The failure of the policy was dramatized in 1999 by the murder of Pfc. Barry Winchell at the hands of Pvt. Calvin Glover, a member of his unit. Glover beat Winchell to death with a baseball bat while he slept. Prosecutors argued that Glover murdered Winchell because he was a homosexual. Glover was sentenced to life in prison. Subsequent inquiries by civilian groups revealed an ongoing pattern of policy violations and antigay harassment that had been ignored by higher-level officers. However, a report by the Army Inspector General exonerated all officers of blame in Winchell's murder and found no climate of homophobia at Fort Campbell, Kentucky, the base where Winchell was bludgeoned to death.

In the wake of the Winchell murder, Hilary Rodham Clinton, Vice-President Al Gore, and even President Clinton labeled the "Don't Ask, Don't Tell" policy a failure. Campaigning for the [2000] Democratic

Party's presidential nomination, candidates Gore and Bill Bradley each promised to work to reverse the policy if he were elected. Meanwhile, candidates for the Republican nomination reaffirmed their support for the current policy (McCain, Bush) or declared that they would seek to completely prohibit military service by homosexuals (Bauer, Keyes, Forbes).

Thus, events in the 2000 political campaigns suggested that the "Don't Ask, Don't Tell" policy—and the broader issue of whether and how gay men and lesbians should serve in the military—remains a volatile issue with great symbolic potency.

# THE LEGAL CONTEXT OF SAME-SEX MARRIAGE IN THE UNITED STATES

NOLO Law for All

Same-sex couples in the United States have been attempting to achieve legal recognition for their unions since the early 1970s. In the new millennium, marriage has resurfaced as a legal goal for same-sex couples. In this selection NOLO Law for All provides the historical and legal context for contemporary gay marriage debates. As NOLO explains, Massachusetts legalized gay marriage in May 2004. In addition, several cities and counties throughout the United States have begun to issue marriage licenses to same-sex couples in the absence of any specific laws forbidding gay marriage. Some states, such as Vermont, Hawaii, New Jersey, and California, have passed legislation to provide same-sex couples with some of the benefits and protections of marriage, without legalizing gay marriage per se. At the same time, opponents of same-sex marriage proposed a federal constitutional amendment along with state-by-state measures to ban gay marriage. NOLO Law for All is a publisher of legal information to enable people to handle their own everyday legal matters. The company currently publishes *A Legal Guide for Lesbian and Gay Couples*.

A common dictionary definition of family is "the basic unit in society having as its nucleus two or more adults living together and cooperating in the care and rearing of their own or adopted children." Despite this all-inclusive definition, a lesbian or gay couple—with or without children—has not been what many people picture when they think of a family.

Nevertheless, lesbian and gay couples (and their children) do live in families and have sought societal recognition of their families over the past several decades. It began in the early 1970s, when same-sex couples applied for marriage licenses, asked courts to allow one partner to adopt the other, and took other stops to legally cement their relationships. Many of these efforts failed, but some progress was made. By the mid 1980s, same-sex couples were seeking domestic partnership recognition from cities and private companies. This effort continued with increasing strength in the 1990s and on into the new century. In recent years, same-sex couples have made enormous strides toward equal recognition of their families.

## Same-Sex Marriage in U.S. Cities

San Francisco Mayor Gavin Newsom really started something on February 12, 2004, when he ordered city clerks to begin issuing marriage licenses to same-sex couples. Since then numerous other U.S. cities have followed his lead, and the entire country's attention has been drawn to the debate. But it will be a while before the issue is settled. Lawsuits in San Francisco and elsewhere are making their way through the courts. . . . All of these legal proceedings will take time, so we're unlikely to have a clear decision any time soon. Meanwhile, the legality of the marriages that have been performed is in question, and it's unclear if those marriages will be recognized outside of the city or county where the licenses were issued.

## Same-Sex Marriage in Massachusetts

The most promising development in the fight for same-sex marriage is the recent Massachusetts Supreme Court decision in *Goodridge v. Department of Public Health* (November 2003). The court held that the state law barring same-sex marriage was unconstitutional under the Massachusetts constitution and ordered the legislature to remedy the discrimination within six months. In February 2004, the court ruled that offering civil unions instead of civil marriage would not meet the requirements set forth in *Goodridge*. As a result, beginning in May 2004, same-sex couples [were] able to get marriage licenses and enter into civil marriages. The Massachusetts legislature is currently considering an amendment to the state constitution to forbid marriage between same-sex couples, but the soonest such an amendment could take effect is 2006.

## Marriage-Like Relationships in Other States

*Vermont: Civil Unions.* In 1999, the Vermont Supreme Court ordered its state legislature to come up with a system providing same-sex couples with traditional marriage benefits and protections. In response to the [Vermont] supreme court mandate [in *Baker v. State*, 1999], the Vermont legislature passed the Vermont Civil Union law, which went into effect on July 1, 2000. While this law doesn't legalize same-sex marriages, it does provide gay and lesbian couples with many of the same advantages, including:

- rights under family laws such as annulment, divorce, child custody, child support, alimony, domestic violence, adoption, and property division

- rights to sue for wrongful death, loss of consortium, and under any other tort or law concerning spousal relationships
- medical rights such as hospital visitation, notification, and durable power of attorney
- family leave benefits
- joint state tax filing, and
- property inheritance when one partner dies without a will.

These rights apply only to couples living in Vermont. But even for Vermont residents this new civil union law does not give same-sex couples the rights and benefits federal law provides to male-female married couples. Same-sex couples are not eligible for Social Security benefits, immigration privileges, or the marriage exemption to federal estate tax. Vermont also permits reciprocal beneficiaries relationships which provide the same health care decision making rights available to spouses and couples in civil unions.

*Hawaii: Reciprocal Beneficiaries.* Hawaii's Reciprocal Beneficiaries law provides some marriage-like benefits. Any two state residents can register as reciprocal beneficiaries, as long as they are over 18 and are not permitted to marry. Couples who sign up gain some of the rights and benefits granted by the state to married couples, including hospital visitation rights, the ability to sue for wrongful death, and property and inheritance rights.

*New Jersey and California: Domestic Partnerships.* New Jersey is the most recent addition to the list of states that offer marriage-like benefits to their citizens. The new domestic partner law, passed in January 2004, applies to same-sex couples and to opposite-sex couples in which one partner is 62 or older. The benefits provided include equality with married couples in insurance coverage and medical decision making and the choice of filing joint state tax returns. However, the law does not provide for inheritance rights, the right to petition for spousal support if the relationship ends, or automatic parental rights— second parents still have to petition for adoption.

In California, the updated domestic partner law gives broad new rights and places extensive new responsibilities on registered partners. As of January 1, 2005, registered domestic partners in California will have many of the same rights and obligations as legally married spouses under state law, including community property rights and the right to receive support from one's partner after a separation. Domestic partners will both be considered legal parents of a child born into the partnership, without the necessity of an adoption. Superior courts will have jurisdiction over termination of domestic partnerships, unless the relationship was of short duration and there are no children and no jointly owned property. There has been significant backlash against the new law, but the opposition has suffered recent setbacks and failed to get enough signatures for a March 2004 ballot referendum that would repeal the law. It's also unclear what legal effect a marriage entered into in San Francisco has on a domestic partnership of the same partners.

## Recognition from State to State

It remains to be seen what effect the laws in California, Hawaii, New Jersey, and Vermont—and same-sex marriages entered into in Massachusetts and in San Francisco and other cities that are issuing marriage licenses—will have on the rest of the nation. Couples that aren't Vermont residents are allowed to register their civil unions in Vermont, but it is doubtful that other states will recognize their status (except New Jersey, where the law explicitly states that it will recognize civil unions and domestic partnerships from other states, and perhaps California and Hawaii). Likewise, California registered domestic partners will probably have trouble having their partnerships recognized anywhere except Hawaii, New Jersey, and Vermont.

Although the U.S. Constitution requires each state to give "full faith and credit" to the laws of other states, the federal Defense of Marriage Act (DOMA), passed in 1996, expressly undercuts the full faith and credit requirement in the case of same-sex marriages. Many states have also passed DOMA laws, specifically barring same-sex marriages in that state. Because of the apparent conflict between the federal DOMA and the U.S. Constitution, as well as all the other uncertainties in this area, equal rights advocates—and their opponents—are eager to have the U.S. Supreme Court decide the issue of same-sex marriage once and for all.

## Chronological History of Same-Sex Marriage Attempts

*Baker v. Nelson* (Minnesota, 1971). A gay male couple argued that the absence of sex-specific language in the Minnesota statute was evidence of the legislature's intent to authorize same-sex marriages. The couple also claimed that prohibiting them from marrying was a denial of their due process and equal protection rights under the Constitution. The court stated that it could find no support for these arguments in any United States Supreme Court decision.

*Jones v. Hallahan* (Kentucky, 1973). A lesbian couple argued that denying them a marriage license deprived them of three basic constitutional rights—the right to marry, the right to associate, and the right to freely exercise their religion. The court refused to address the constitutional issues, holding that "the relationship proposed does not authorize the issuance of a marriage license, because what they propose is not a marriage."

*Singer v. Hara* (Washington, 1974). A gay male couple argued that denying them the right to marry violated the state Equal Rights Amendment. The court disagreed, holding that the purpose of the statute was to overcome discriminatory legal treatment between men and women on account of sex.

*Adams v. Howerton* (Colorado, 1975). The couple, a male American citizen and a male Australian citizen, challenged the Board of Immigration Appeals refusal to recognize their marriage for the purpose of the Australian obtaining U.S. residency as the spouse of an American. (The couple participated in a marriage ceremony with a Colorado minister and had been granted a marriage license by the Boulder, Colorado county clerk.) The court ruled that the word "spouse" ordinarily means someone not of the same sex. Then it noted the 1965 amendments to the Immigration Act, which expressly barred persons "afflicted with sexual deviations" (homosexuals) from entry into this country. The court concluded that it was unlikely that Congress intended to permit homosexual marriages for purposes of qualifying as a spouse of a citizen, when the Immigration Act explicitly bars homosexuals from entering into the United States.

*Thorton v. Timmers* (Ohio, 1975). A lesbian couple sought a marriage license. In denying their request that the court order the clerk to issue them a license, the court concluded that "it is the express legislative intent that those persons who may be joined in marriage must be of different sexes."

*De Santo v. Barnsley* (Pennsylvania, 1984). When this couple split up, De Santo sued Barnsley for divorce, claiming that the couple had a common-law marriage. A common-law marriage is one where the partners live together and act as a married couple, without going through a formal marriage ceremony. Only a few states still recognize common-law marriages—in 1984 Pennsylvania was one of those states. The court threw the case out, stating that if the Pennsylvania common-law statute is to be expanded to include same-sex couples, the legislature will have to make that change.

*Matter of Estate of Cooper* (New York, 1990). Cooper died, leaving the bulk of his property to his ex-lover. His current lover sued to inherit as a surviving spouse under New York's inheritance laws. The court concluded that only a lawfully recognized husband or wife qualifies as a surviving spouse and that "persons of the same sex have no constitutional rights to enter into a marriage with each other."

*Dean v. District of Columbia* (Washington, DC, 1995). Two men sued the District of Columbia for the right to get married. They lost their case at the lower level and appealed. They lost again at the appellate level when the court decided, under current D.C. laws, that the district can refuse to grant marriage licenses to same-sex couples.

*Baehr v. Miike* (Hawaii, 1999). A nine-year battle over the issue of same-sex marriages ended just 11 days before the Vermont ruling in *Baker v. State*, discussed below. The plaintiff in the *Baehr* case argued that Hawaii's marriage license rules were discriminatory. The case set off a national debate over same-sex marriage rights and prompted an onslaught of state and federal legislation designed to preempt the possibility that other states would be forced to recognize same-sex marriages from Hawaii. The case was finally dismissed on the grounds that the legislature had passed a prohibition on same-sex marriages before the Hawaii Supreme Court could render a favorable opinion.

*Baker v. State* (Vermont, 1999). Same-sex couples sued the state, the City of Burlington, and two towns, saying that refusal to issue them marriage licenses violated the Vermont Constitution and the state marriage laws. The Vermont Supreme Court, reversing a lower court decision, declared that the constitution required the state to extend to same-sex couples the same benefits and protections provided to opposite-sex couples. In response, the state legislature passed the Vermont Civil Union law, which went into effect in July 2000.

*Goodridge v. Department of Public Health* (Massachusetts, 2003). The Massachusetts Supreme Court held that the state law barring same-sex marriage was unconstitutional under the Massachusetts constitution and ordered the legislature to remedy the discrimination within six months. In February 2004, the court ruled that offering civil unions instead of civil marriage would not meet the requirements set forth in *Goodridge*.

# Overturning Antisodomy Legislation: The History of *Lawrence v. Texas*

Wikipedia

*Lawrence v. Texas* was a landmark case in the history of gay rights. On November 20, 1998, John Geddes Lawrence and Tyron Garner were convicted of violating Texas's antisodomy "homosexual conduct" law. Lawrence and Garner appealed the decision until the case arrived at the U.S. Supreme Court in 2002. On June 26, 2003, the Supreme Court overturned the lower court's decision and declared the homosexual conduct law to be unconstitutional. The decision was a victory for gay rights activists and may eventually have broader implications for legal decisions about liberty, privacy, and due process. The next selection from Wikipedia describes the history of *Lawrence v. Texas* and its indications. Wikipedia is a free online encyclopedia.

*Lawrence v. Texas* was a 2003 case decided by the United States Supreme Court. In the 6-3 ruling, the justices invalidated the criminal prohibition of homosexual sodomy in Texas. The court had previously addressed the same issue in 1986 with *Bowers v. Hardwick*, but there had upheld the challenged Georgia statute, not finding a constitutional right to homosexual sodomy.

*Lawrence*, case number 02-102, explicitly overturned *Bowers*, which it held viewed the liberty at stake too narrowly. The *Lawrence* court held that intimate consensual sexual conduct was part of the liberty protected by substantive due process under the Fourteenth Amendment.

*Lawrence* had the effect of invalidating similar laws throughout the United States insofar as they apply to consenting adults acting in private. The case attracted much public attention, and a large number of amicus curiae ("friend of the court") briefs were filed in the case. The decision, which contained a bold declaration of the dignity of homosexual persons, was celebrated by gay rights activists, hoping that further legal advances may result as a consequence; the decision was lamented by social conservatives for the same reasons.

Wikipedia, "*Lawrence v. Texas*," http://en.wikipedia.org, July 18, 2004.

## History of the Case

The petitioners, medical technologist John Geddes Lawrence, 60, and street-stand barbecue vendor Tyron Garner, 36, were found having consensual anal sex in Lawrence's suburban apartment in the suburbs of Houston between 10:30 and 11 P.M. on September 17, 1998 when Harris County sheriff's deputy Joseph Quinn entered the unlocked apartment with his weapon drawn, arresting the two.

The arrests had stemmed from a false report of a "weapons disturbance" in their home—that because of a domestic disturbance or robbery, there was a man with a gun "going crazy." The person who filed the report, neighbor Roger David Nance, 41, had earlier been accused of harassing the plaintiffs. (Despite the false report, probable cause to enter the home was not at issue in the case; Nance later admitted that he was lying and pled no contest to charges of filing a false police report and served 15 days in jail).

Lawrence and Garner were arrested, held overnight in jail, and charged with violating Texas's anti-sodomy statute, the Texas "Homosexual Conduct" law. The law, Chapter 21, Sec. 21.01 of the Texas Penal Code, provides that it is a Class C misdemeanor for someone to "engage in deviate sexual intercourse with another individual of the same sex," apparently prohibiting anal and oral sex between members of the same sex, but not between members of the opposite sex. They later posted $200 bail.

On November 20, Lawrence and Garner pleaded no contest to the charges. They were convicted by Justice of the Peace Mike Parrott, but exercised their right to a new trial before a Texas Criminal Court, where they asked the court to dismiss the charges against them on Fourteenth Amendment equal protection grounds, claiming that the law was not constitutional since it prohibits sodomy between same-sex couples but not between heterosexual couples, and also on right to privacy grounds (also known as the "substantive due process" argument).

This said that the right to privacy for heterosexual couples had previously been recognized to include sex, including sex using contraception, (i.e., non-procreative sex, but not sodomy). After the Criminal Court rejected this request, they pleaded no contest, reserving their right to file an appeal, and were fined $125 each (out of a maximum fine of $500 each), plus $141.25 in court costs.

On November 4, 1999, arguments were presented to a three-judge panel of the 14th Court of Appeals on both equal protection and right to privacy grounds. John S. Anderson and chief justice Paul Murphy ruled in the defendants' favor, finding that the law violated the 1972 Equal Rights Amendment to the Texas constitution, which bars discrimination because of of sex, race, color, creed or national origin. J. Harvey Hudson dissented. This 2-1 decision ruled the Texas law was unconstitutional; the full court, however, voted to reconsider its decision, upholding the law's constitutionality 7-2 and denying both the substantive due process and the equal protection arguments. On April 13, 2001, the Texas Court of Criminal Appeals, was petitioned to hear the case; the Court, the highest appellate court in Texas, denied review. The case then arrived at the Supreme Court, with a petition being filed July 16, 2002.

## Considerations

The Supreme Court granted a *writ of certiorari* [to procure records from the lower court] agreeing to hear the case on July 16, 2002. Widely varying organizations filed *amicus curiae* [friend of the court] briefs on behalf of the petitioners:

- The American Bar Association;
- The National Lesbian and Gay Law Association, et al.;
- Constitutional Law Professors, Bruce Ackerman, et al.;
- The American Civil Liberties Union and ACLU of Texas;
- The American Psychological Association, et al.;
- The Republican Unity Coalition, Alan K. Simpson, the Log Cabin Republicans and Liberty Education Reform;
- The Alliance of Baptists, et al.;
- The Cato Institute and Institute for Justice;
- The National Organization for Women; NOW Legal Defense and Education Fund;
- American Public Health Association, et al.;
- Mary Robinson, et al.;
- Professors of History, George Chauncey, et al.; and
- Human Rights Campaign, et al.

Oral argument was heard in the case on March 26, 2003; the decision was rendered on June 26, 2003.

The questions before the court were the following:

1. Whether the petitioners' criminal convictions under the Texas "Homosexual Conduct" law—which criminalizes sexual intimacy by same-sex couples, but not identical behavior by different-sex couples—violate the Fourteenth Amendment guarantee of equal protection of the laws;
2. Whether the petitioners' criminal convictions for adult consensual sexual intimacy in their home violate their vital interests in liberty and privacy protected by the Due Process Clause of the Fourteenth Amendment; and
3. Whether *Bowers v. Hardwick* should be overruled.

## The Decision

The Supreme Court voted 6-3 to strike down the Texas law, with the five-justice majority saying it violated due process guarantees. The majority opinion, which reverses *Bowers v. Hardwick*, appears to cover similar laws in 12 other states. Justice Anthony Kennedy wrote the majority opinion; Justices John Paul Stevens, David Souter, Ruth Bader

Ginsburg and Stephen Breyer joined. The court stated that, as part of constitutionally protected liberty, homosexuals have "the full right to engage in private conduct without government intervention."

The decision cited the 1981 case *Dudgeon v. United Kingdom*, a case heard by the European Court of Human Rights, as demonstrating in part that the court's assumption in *Bowers* (that Western civilization uniformly condemned homosexuality) was erroneous, and added that "*Bowers* was not correct when it was decided, and was not correct at that time. It ought not to remain binding precedent. *Bowers v. Hardwick* should be and now is overruled."

The majority decision found that the intimate, adult consensual conduct at issue here was part of the liberty protected by the substantive component of the Fourteenth Amendment's due process protections. Holding that "[t]he Texas statute furthers no legitimate state interest which can justify its intrusion into the personal and private life of the individual," the court struck down the anti-sodomy law as unconstitutional.

Justice Sandra Day O'Connor filed a concurring opinion, agreeing with the invalidation of the sodomy law but not with Kennedy's rationale. O'Connor disagreed with both the overturning of *Bowers* (in which she was in the majority) and with the court's invocation of due process guarantees of liberty in this context. O'Connor instead preferred the more limited equal protection argument which would still strike the law because it was directed against a group rather than an act, but would avoid the inclusion of sexuality under protected liberty.

Under this argument, O'Connor maintained that a sodomy law that was neutral both in effect and application might well be constitutional, but that there was little to fear because "democratic society" would not tolerate it for long. She did leave the door open for laws which distinguished between homosexuals and heterosexuals on the basis of legitimate state interest, but found that this was not such a law.

Justice Antonin Scalia wrote a sharply worded dissent, in which Chief Justice William H. Rehnquist and Justice Clarence Thomas joined. Scalia objected to the Court's decision to revisit *Bowers*, pointing out that there were many subsequent decisions from lower courts based on *Bowers* that, with its overturning, may now be open to doubt:

> *Williams v. Pryor*, which upheld Alabama's prohibition on the sale of sex toys; *Milner v. Apfel*, which asserted that "legislatures are permitted to legislate with regard to morality . . . rather than confined to preventing demonstrable harms;" *Holmes v. California Army National Guard*, which upheld the federal statute and regulations banning from military service those who engage in homosexual conduct; *Owens v. State*, which held that "a person has no constitutional right to engage in sexual intercourse, at least outside of marriage."

Echoing Senator Rick Santorum's May 2003 comments, the dissenting justices stated that the majority's findings would lead to a "right to bigamy, you have the right to polygamy, you have the right to incest, you have the right to adultery, you have the right to anything," Scalia also claimed that "State laws against bigamy, same-sex marriage, adult incest, prostitution, masturbation, adultery, fornication, bestiality, and obscenity are likewise sustainable only in light of *Bowers'* validation of laws based on moral choices."

Scalia asserted that with this decision, the Court "has largely signed on to the so-called homosexual agenda," adding that he has "nothing against homosexuals, or any other group, promoting their agenda through normal democratic means."

Justice Thomas, in a separate short opinion, wrote that the law which the Court struck down was "uncommonly silly" but that he voted to uphold it as he could find no general right of privacy or relevant liberty in the Constitution.

## Broader Implications

*Lawrence v. Texas* may eventually come to be seen as one of the most important decisions by the United States Supreme Court. The broader implications of the Court's decision include the following:

- Though not decided upon equal protection grounds, the majority decision still calls into question other legal limitations on the rights of homosexuals, including the right to state recognition of homosexual marriages, and the right to serve in the military.
- An issue central to the case, particularly focused on during oral argument, was whether laws can be justified merely through invocations of "morality" without the demonstration of any actual harm. This issue was a major concern for Justice Scalia in his dissent. Many laws would likely fail the test that the Texas sodomy statute failed here, including those prohibiting other forms of sexual behavior considered "deviant," or bans against obscene materials.
- This case and its opinions exemplify fundamental debates in constitutional theory. Some argue that the original intent of the framers of the constitution should play the central role in constitutional interpretation. Others argue that the courts should have a more active role in expanding concepts of liberty, striking down majoritarian law when necessary to protect unsympathetic minority groups and conduct. Both general positions have their judicial and scholarly supporters.
- Central to the conflict over constitutional interpretation is the doctrine of *substantive due process*, a doctrine that protects rights not explicitly guaranteed in the Constitution but still considered "implicit in ordered liberty." The doctrine has been used throughout most of the court's history, typically to protect rights tradi-

tionally recognized as central to American society, such as those relating to marriage and the raising of children. However, many of its applications have been the target of criticism that the justices have read their personal views into the Constitution (see, for example, *Lochner v. New York*). The right to privacy, particularly in the context of abortion, is considered by some contemporary critics to be just such an unwarranted and excessive judicial invention. In light of this, it may be significant that Justice Kennedy's majority opinion focused on *liberty* rather than *privacy*. Though both are embraced under substantive due process, the shift might signal a significant change in the theoretical basis of the Court's fundamental rights jurisprudence, perhaps in an attempt to skirt the usual criticism over a general privacy right (see due process).

- The use of European court decisions as persuasive authority by the majority in the United States raises the question of what influence foreign court decisions should have on United States law. Generally, conservatives (whether judicial or social) vehemently object to the use of foreign court decisions as any kind of authority. Many thinkers of a more liberal bent believe that the U.S. should accommodate itself to international norms, and that foreign decisions, especially those from Europe, should have at least persuasive influence on U.S. jurisprudence.

As with all Supreme Court cases, the meaning of *Lawrence* will deepen as it is interpreted by lower state and federal courts, legal scholars, and the Supreme Court itself, revealing how broad or how narrow its guarantees of liberty extend.

# CHAPTER 4

# CULTURAL, RELIGIOUS, AND MORAL ISSUES

# LESBIANS AND GAYS ARE GAINING VISIBILITY IN POPULAR CULTURE

Joshua Gamson

The popular culture of earlier decades tended to ignore homosexuality altogether or to stigmatize gay life as scary, tragic, and deviant. In recent years, however, images of gays and lesbians in mainstream popular culture have mushroomed. One of the reasons for this is that the corporate world has finally realized that the gay and lesbian community is a lucrative market niche. As Joshua Gamson explains in this selection, critics disagree about whether this new visibility in mainstream America is positive for gay and lesbian people. Critics argue that the portrayals of gays and lesbians are "sanitized images" that emphasize the similarities and standards that they share with heterosexual people, implying that only homosexuals who are indistinguishable from heterosexuals are acceptable. The depictions also tend to focus on white, affluent gays, ignoring the diversity of gay and lesbian populations and the difficulties they face. There is also no evidence that the new cultural visibility is helping gays and lesbians gain political rights. Gamson is a professor of sociology at the University of San Francisco and the author of *Freaks Talk Back: Tabloid Talk Shows and Sexual Nonconformity*.

'The big lie about lesbians and gay men,' the late Vito Russo wrote in *The Celluloid Closet*, his 1980s' landmark study of homosexuality in the movies, 'is that we do not exist.'

America was a dream that had no room for the existence of homosexuals. Laws were made against depicting such things on screen. And when the fact of our existence became unavoidable, we were reflected, on screen and off, as dirty secrets. We have cooperated for a very long time in the maintenance of our own invisibility. And now the party is over.

Indeed. By the start of the twenty-first century, gay and lesbian charac-

Joshua Gamson, "Sweating in the Spotlight: Lesbian, Gay and Queer Encounters with Media and Popular Culture," *Handbook of Lesbian and Gay Studies*, edited by Diane Richardson and Steven Seidman. Thousand Oaks, CA: Sage, 2002. Copyright © 2002 by Joshua Gamson. Reproduced by permission of Sage Publications, Ltd.

ters were all over American popular culture and, at least most of the time, neither secret nor particularly dirty. Gays and lesbians now routinely appear in US mainstream newspaper and popular magazine coverage, often sympathetically or matter-of-factly; entertainment and sports stars such as Ellen DeGeneres, Anne Heche, Greg Louganis, Martina Navratilova, Ian McKellen, Rupert Everett, and Melissa Etheridge are out and about in American culture, gracing magazine covers and celebrity gossip news; gay, lesbian, bisexual, and transgendered characters abound in Hollywood films and independent films too numerous to list, and have appeared as lead and recurring characters on many television programs, from the famous *Ellen* coming-out episode to *Will and Grace, Dawson's Creek, Felicity, NYPD Blue*, and *South Park*, to name just a few; major companies such as Ikea, Budweiser, United Airlines, Subaru, and American Express have targeted gay and lesbian consumers with flattering images of themselves, often published in slick gay and lesbian magazines or on well-trafficked gay and lesbian Internet sites. Even Disney World has an annual gay event.

Although the effects of such cultural changes on public opinion—which has become increasingly supportive of lesbian and gay civil equality while remaining morally disapproving—are never direct or obvious, the shifts have been stunning in both breadth and rapidity. As Suzanna Danuta Walters puts it in *All the Rage*, a scant twenty years after Russo, 'the love that dare not speak its name became the love that would not shut up.' . . .

## Gays and Lesbians in the Media

'The most effective force of resistance to the hegemonic force of the dominant media,' communications scholar Larry Gross wrote, 'is to speak for oneself,' and 'the ultimate expression of independence for a minority audience struggling to free itself from the dominant culture's hegemony is to become the creators and not merely the consumers of media images.' For a time in the earlier parts of the contemporary gay and lesbian movements' history, much energy had been devoted to creating alternative institutions, some of which gave rise to an alternative popular culture by and for gay people: lesbian feminist singers recorded on the Olivia Records label and played at the Michigan Womyn's Music Festival, local papers emerged, along with national magazines such as *The Advocate*, to provide news and information that the mainstream press ignored or distorted; gay-produced films such as *Word Is Out, The Times of Harvey Milk*, and *Tongues Untied* documented aspects of gay experience, and played at lesbian and gay film festivals.

Until recently, however, the cultural images gays and lesbians produced were known and distributed mostly within lesbian and gay communities, and the images in the popular culture at large were produced by and for heterosexual audiences—although, of course, homosexuals were among their most avid consumers. Over time, in a process that began slowly in the 1970s, picked up over the 1980s, and sped up like crazy in the 1990s, the volume of mainstream popular culture featuring gays and lesbians, and of gay- or lesbian-produced culture 'crossing over' into the culture at large, mushroomed dramatically.

## Gay Money

In large part, this newfound visibility was, in fact, the result of the erosion of corporate caution about being associated with gay and lesbian culture, which opened up big new revenue and investment sources for cultural products featuring, or targeting, gays and lesbians. The gay and lesbian 'community' had, largely through the efforts of some of its own (for instance, firms specifically geared towards helping companies market towards gay and lesbian consumers), been transformed into a market niche. Although various studies have challenged the idea that gay men and lesbians earn more than heterosexuals, and statistics on stigmatized populations are notoriously difficult to collect, the perception that lesbians and gay men are a huge, untapped, brand-loyal group with lots of disposable income began to become conventional business wisdom. Thus major advertisers, such as airlines and music companies and alcohol companies, sought ways to penetrate the gay market. One of those ways was through gay-and-lesbian produced popular culture, especially the glossy magazines such as *Out, 10 Percent, Genre,* and *Curve,* which emerged in the 1990s, and long-standing magazines such as *The Advocate.* 'The growing visibility of the gay and lesbian community,' as [author] Michael Bronski put it, 'has been largely a direct result of the emergence of the gay market and the commodification of gay life.'

The visibility grew not only in print advertising and magazines. The decreased perception of financial risk on the part of corporations loosened up investment in gay- and lesbian-themed film and television projects, and a series of test cases proved that they could be profitable. The AIDS drama *Philadelphia* demonstrated that audiences might not turn away from Hollywood films with gay central characters; the indie film *Go Fish,* which centered around a group of twenty-something lesbians, became a hit in 1996, demonstrating that films emerging from the budding gay and lesbian independent film world could be highly profitable. The episode in which the title character of *Ellen* came out proved to be a ratings bonanza, demolishing the idea that gay topics were too controversial to retain TV viewers' valuable attention—which had informed earlier advertiser pullouts from episodes of television shows, such as *LA Law* and *Roseanne,* in which same-sex desire was a key storyline, and which had kept networks from supporting programs with gay or lesbian lead characters. Film companies became less cautious about producing and marketing gay-themed films, distributors were on the lookout for independently produced films about lesbian and gay characters that had 'crossover' potential, and advertisers became less skittish about sponsoring television programs with lesbian or gay characters. By the late 1980s, the 'funding, production, and distribution opportunities' for people pursuing lesbian and gay themes in independent media, and the field of lesbian and gay film and video itself, were 'expanding, exploring, exploding' [according to the authors of *Queer Looks: Perspectives on Lesbian and Gay Film and Video*]; lesbian and gay cultural producers who a few years before would have been ignored found eager commercial sponsors and distributors. Lesbian and gay images have made a fast march towards the center of American popular culture. 'Gay life and identity,' as sociologist Susannah Walters says, 'defined so much by the problems of invisibility, subliminal coding, double entendres and double lives, has now taken on the dubious distinction of public spectacle.'

Very few observers dispute the claim that the recent pop cultural visibility of gays and lesbians has primarily taken the form of emphasizing gay people's similarity to their heterosexual counterparts, that as opposed to their stereotyping as scary, deviant 'others' in the years preceding it, they have become increasingly 'normal' cultural figures. Even their deviance, in fact, has become normalized: gays and lesbians, who had been relegated to occasional talk show appearances in the 1970s and 1980s on which the morality of their practices and identities was the topic, for example, were in the 1990s integrated into the tabloid world of daytime talk shows, as nasty and loud as most everyone else on the shows.

## Good or Bad?

What scholars and other observers disagree about, however, is whether and how the new visibility is a cause for celebration. For students of media and popular culture, the mainstreaming of lesbian and gay people in the late twentieth and early twenty-first century has generated new questions, and reproduced once again the political tension between those advocating assimilation and normalization as routes to social progress and those pursuing a 'queer' challenge to norms as a social change strategy. For more conservative critics, the new visibility is progress, a sign that the culture at large is getting over its stereotypes and ignorance and accepting gay people. In *After the Ball: How America Will Conquer Its Fear and Hatred of Gays in the 90s*, for instance, Marshall Kirk and Hunter Madsen described a strategy of 'good propaganda' that seemed to then play out almost as if drawn from their pages. In a reiteration of a conformity-oriented strategy with a long history in gay politics, they proposed producing 'favorably sanitized images' and a 'single-minded' focus on 'gay rights issues and nothing more.'

> You must help them relate to you and your humanity, to recognize that you and they share many good things in common, and that they can like and accept you *on their own terms.*

> . . . Persons featured in the media campaign should be whole-some and admirable by *straight standards*, and completely unexceptional in appearance; in a word, they should be *indistinguishable from the straights* we'd like to reach. In practical terms, this means that cocky mustachioed leathermen, drag queens, and bull dykes would not appear in gay commercial and other public presentations.

This is exactly one of the major objections to others witnessing the movement of gays and lesbians into the mainstream of popular culture. 'Far too often this new visibility and acceptance,' writes Walters, 'is predicated on a comparative model: the straight person (or character in a film or TV show) can only "accept" the gay person once he or she has interpreted that person as "just like me."' Normalization, some critics have pointed out, comes at a price, the need to 'tone down, clean up, straighten up gay life and gay identity,' a neglect of the diversity of gay populations, and a writing out of the sexually transgressive and politically challenging aspects of the lesbian and gay communities and movements.

Most critical analysts point to the distortions provided by the commodification of gay and lesbian life, the driving force behind the new cultural visibility. 'Not only is much recent gay visibility aimed at producing new and potentially lucrative markets, but as in most marketing strategies, money, not liberation, is the bottom line,' writes [scholar] Rosemary Hennessy. 'The increasing circulation of gay and lesbian images in consumer culture has the effect of consolidating an imaginary, class-specific gay subjectivity for both straight and gay audiences.' The overwhelming majority of advertising material in which gay people appear, [author] Alexandra Chasin has found, for instance, depicts that "community" as white, affluent, educated, healthy, youngish adults.' 'In the world of the market,' Walters adds, 'all the gays are men, all the men are white, and all the whites are rich.' Recent gay magazines, cultural critic Daniel Harris argues in *The Rise and Fall of Gay Culture*, 'have consolidated their economic base by catering exclusively to the needs of the emerging youth constituency and perpetrating pictorial genocide on men over the age of 40, who have been ethnically cleansed from their pages, leaving behind a racially pure group of young, prosperous beauties.' Gay activism, he continues, has been redefined to include 'things like shopping and careering,' and images of gay culture 'have been completely desexualized.' The new magazines, Harris argues:

> strive to create a sanitized forum that will satisfy even the most conservative businesses. . . . [Editors] drive home to their advertisers the normality of gay people whose Middle American mediocrity is celebrated in article after article. . . . The methods of sterilization involved in creating an ad-friendly

marketing vehicle capable of pacifying the fears of large corporations involves the annihilation of gay identity, the eradication of every vestige of difference between ourselves and
the heterosexual markets the advertiser is accustomed to
addressing.

The new visibility, the more radical observers suggest, has brought
new distortions. At a minimum, the move of some gay people into
the cultural mainstream has heightened the tension between assimilationist and anti-assimilationist wings in gay politics.

It has also called attention to analytical and political difficulties
that were not present when the task was simply documenting and
opposing images that were blatantly demeaning. The assumption that
a 'positive' image is easily recognizable, is no longer so easy to hold.
'Is it any image that avoids the harshest stereotypes?' asks [scholar]
Jane Schacter.

Is it a highly assimilated image that makes it impossible to
'tell' if someone is straight or gay? Is it an image that attrib-
utes transgressive gender roles to a gay character—an 'effeminate' man or 'masculine' woman—but does so from a 'sympathetic' perspective? It is simply any such 'transgressive' image,
available for a potentially empowering appropriation by lesbian and gay viewers, irrespective of the ways in which non-
gay viewers might react?

These are questions triggered by the move into the spotlight of popular culture, and their answers are primarily normative ones—they
depend on where one stands on the *value* of transgression, assimilation, and normalization.

## Looking to the Future

These are never bad questions to ask, not least because gay people's
ambivalent relationship to media and popular culture—as stigmatizing enemy and destigmatizing savior—is productive. They also force
new and difficult issues, about the politics of visibility, into the forefront of the field. It is no longer so easy to assume that visibility, for
instance, is always and necessarily a political step forward. The means
by which much of the new cultural visibility was achieved—the promotion of an affluent, powerful gay market—has become one of the
organizing tools for the anti-gay right, for instance. Now, as Michael
Bronski sums up the results of these 'myths created by means of market research,' gay people are seen by some not just as a sexual threat,
but 'a sexual threat with economic and social power.' 'It is at least
possible,' Schacter points out:

that representations of happy, healthy, well integrated lesbian
and gay characters in film or television would create the im-

pression that, in a social, economic, and legal sense, all is well for lesbians and gay men. To the extent that some viewers believe that media images reflect the 'real world,' perhaps these images will induce or confirm their belief that lesbians and gay men are already 'equal'—accepted, integrated, part of the mainstream. . . . It is at least possible that 'positive' images of gay and lesbian characters, untethered to any representation of the legal status of homosexuality, might prompt in some viewers the rallying cry of 'special rights' that has been so central to the antigay campaigns.

There is, thus far, no indication that new cultural visibility translates into new political and social rights and fuller, freer citizenship for gay people. Indeed, the impact of popular culture on political opinion, the impact of this new visibility—whether the exposure has generated tolerance or backlash—remains to be seen and studied.

That is a difficult question to transform into research, of course, but its prominence calls attention to one of the largest gaps in the field of lesbian and gay media and pop-culture studies: the dearth of cross-cultural comparison. . . . Most of the work in the field has focused on North American and British culture, not surprisingly, since those are arguably the sites with the most active and visible gay and lesbian presence in popular culture. Especially as world culture continues to compress, and cultural industries continue to consolidate and globalize, it becomes even more crucial to look beyond the American and British cases alone for clues to the difficult, less-than-obvious relationship between cultural visibility and political freedom.

# HOMOPHOBIA IS RAMPANT IN PROFESSIONAL SPORTS

Dave Ford

The male-dominated culture of sports and sportswriting can be a hostile environment for gay men. In this selection Dave Ford reports on *Boston Herald* sports columnist Ed Gray's public declaration of his homosexuality—an action Gray took to openly confront what he believes is the last bastion of prejudice and discrimination in sports. Ford explores possible reasons why homophobia is so prevalent in the world of sports, including the hypermasculine image of athletes, the tendency for coaches to try to shame athletes by calling them "sissies" or "girls," and unacknowledged homoeroticism in locker rooms. Ford agrees with Gray that the time has come to initiate discussions about ending homophobia in the field of sports.

There comes a time for most gay, lesbian, bisexual and transgender people when it's right to set aside the lying, shame and despair haunting life in the closet. For some it happens early; for others, later. It is done in different contexts (conversations, e-mails, phone calls) and stages (parents might be told first, or, indeed, last). It is rarely easy, yet is almost always satisfying.

For longtime *Boston Herald* sports columnist and general assignment sports reporter Ed Gray, that time came last Tuesday. The place was on the back page of the 250,000-circulation daily morning tabloid.

"I'm out," Gray wrote in his column, "because I no longer, in good conscience, choose to ignore the unabashed homophobia that is so cavalierly tolerated within the world of sports." That was in the third paragraph of the 13-paragraph piece, and set a tone with which Gray would determinedly stick in a phone interview later that day.

"The sports world is going nowhere as far as this issue, and it's amazing—it truly is like the gay community is the last minority that is fair game to bigotry and prejudice," he told me. "It's just gotten to a point where I just couldn't be quiet about it any more—and I'm not a person who likes to draw attention to himself."

As in any male-dominated culture in which men are in close physical contact and "masculinity" is prized above all, homophobia in professional sports runs rampant (more in some sports than in others).

It's obvious in occasional player comments, such as when San Francisco 49er Garrison Hearst last year told a *Fresno Bee* reporter, "I don't want any faggots on my team." More subtly, it exists when teams and leagues allow half-hearted player apologies for such gaffes to substitute for true ethical change.

While using his coming out column to highlight the issue, Gray, 55, and a 20-year *Herald* veteran, repeatedly deflected questions about his personal life, appearing diffident about positioning himself a hero.

"It's not about me," he says. "It's about my message."

He noted, however, that he has solid support among colleagues, friends and family.

Said *Herald* editor Andrew F. Costello, "I thought it was courageous of Ed to talk about that issue, especially when it involves him personally." He added, "I hope this opens the door for others to talk about this."

Steven Petrow, president of the National Lesbian and Gay Journalists Association, agreed, especially "for a man to declare he's gay, then go to work in one of the most exclusively male spheres."

Robert Lipsyte, a former full-time sportswriter and a contributor on culture, city issues and sports at *The New York Times*, says that, as far as he knows, Gray's coming out is a first among sportswriters.

## Causes of Sports Homophobia

In a phone interview last week from his New York home, Lipsyte said players' homophobia often traces to coaches of boys and young men who, he says, "use shame and humiliation to get short-term gains, and keep (young players) in line by calling them girl, faggot, sissy."

Some gay boys are driven out of sports for good in high school or college; the few who remain to play in pro sports keep a tight lid on their sexuality.

But Gray, with the optimism of someone who has just released himself from years in a self-imposed prison, says he sees that changing soon. "I think somebody can come out on a major team and survive," he says, noting that the move would require team support—which, eventually, would translate to fan support. "No one's ever tried."

The red-herring fear that dominates the coming-out-in-sports conversation centers, of course, on the locker room. As Petrow puts it, "Even though it's the 21st century, these locker rooms can be antediluvian."

Many heterosexual men evince displeasure at the idea of gay guys showering with them. The implied fear is that gay men, apparently unable to control their impulses, will hurl themselves upon the unsuspecting straight guy, swiping his virginity before he can say "Billy

Bean."[1] (This same sort of attitude resulted in then-ABC and *Sports Illustrated* reporter Melissa Ludtke to sue major league baseball in 1978 for access after being shut out of locker rooms during the previous year's World Series, paving the way for female reporters in that all-male bastion.)

The idea that gay men will attack other men is, of course, is whack —yet may be heightened, Lipsyte notes, by the kinds of locker room horseplay between players that, to outsiders, looks decidedly homoerotic.

"They're always grabbing each others' d-s and slapping each other's butts," he said, "and some of this is very exciting for them." But, he added, as with incarcerated straight-identified men who have sex with men, "Whatever you call it, these guys who engage in what would be called, quote, homosexual acts don't define themselves as homosexual."

It stands to reason, then, that a man comfortable with his homosexuality would threaten this secret society by forcing others to face up to their own male-male leanings. Thus would it call into question the very notion of sports-culture masculinity, to which weakness (read: femininity, in players' minds) is anathema. "The facade of strength is so important," Lipsyte says.

It is possible, some observers suggest, that Gray himself—who mostly covers horse racing, but also files color stories on the New England Patriots and occasionally covers college football—might encounter resistance when next he enters a locker room.

"If indeed that sense of masculinity in the locker room—and I believe this is the case in jock culture—is so fragile," Lipsyte said, "then they will be threatened by him coming in, and they will make remarks."

Gray, however, professes to care little. "It's not even an issue," he said, adding, "I think this whole locker room thing is this irrational fear that's been festering, and that's part of why I needed to talk. Most fear, there's no basis to it."

That's why Gray plans to carry on doing what he's done for decades: write about sports—free, now, of past chains.

"I'm totally comfortable," he says. "I totally respect people's feelings, and I really assume that they respect mine."

1. Billy Bean is a former San Diego Padres outfielder who came out as gay after he retired from professional baseball in 1995.

# CAN HOMOSEXUALS BECOME HETEROSEXUAL?: THE REPARATIVE THERAPY CONTROVERSY

Kenneth J. Zucker

Reparative therapy is a controversial form of psychological treatment used to change a person's sexual orientation from homosexual to heterosexual. In this selection Kenneth J. Zucker surveys the political and scientific viewpoints that inform the contentious debate over the safety and effectiveness of reparative therapy. Zucker notes that since the American Psychiatric Association declared that homosexuality would no longer be considered a mental disorder, very few mental health professionals are trying to help people change their sexual orientation. However, in the 1990s a group of mental health scholars asserted that reparative therapy was useful for some homosexuals. Little thorough and credible research has been done to support or discredit claims by practitioners who claim to be able to transform gays and lesbians into heterosexuals. Zucker calls for more researchers to study reparative therapy and its effects. Zucker is director of the Child and Adolescent Gender Identity Clinic at the University of Toronto's Centre for Addiction and Mental Health. He is a professor of psychiatry and the author of *Gender Identity Disorder and Psychosexual Problems in Children and Adolescents.*

It is now 30 years since the American Psychiatric Association deleted homosexuality per se as a mental disorder from the second edition of the *Diagnostic and Statistical Manual of Mental Disorders* [DSM] (American Psychiatric Association, 1968). . . . Prior to this diagnostic migration from abnormality to normality, the literature was replete with various treatment approaches designed to alter a person's same-sex sexual orientation. Although the [1980] DSM-III contained the diagnosis of Ego-Dystonic Homosexuality (which was subsequently deleted from the DSM-III-R [in 1987]), reports of sexual orientation change treat-

Kenneth J. Zucker, "The Politics and Science of 'Reparative Therapy,'" *Archives of Sexual Behavior*, vol. 32, October 2003. Copyright © 2003 by the Plenum Publishing Corporation. Reproduced by permission of Springer Science and Business Media and the author.

ments began to wane and gradually [were] replaced by various therapeutic approaches designed to be more "affirmative" in helping an individual adapt to a same-sex sexual orientation and to address an array of identified unique needs of gay and lesbian clients.

Although it is well-known that not all mental health professionals agreed with the decision to remove homosexuality from the DSM, it is clear that only a small minority of contemporary practitioners still regard homosexuality per se as pathological. Matters of diagnostics aside, it is also clear that, like their heterosexual counterparts, gays and lesbians seek out therapy for all kinds of reasons. Indeed, there is even one scholarly journal, *Journal of Gay and Lesbian Psychotherapy*, devoted specifically to gay and lesbian therapeutics.

In the early 1990s, a "movement" of clinical dissenters appeared on the scene. They argued that there were some clients with a homosexual sexual orientation who, for various reasons, wished to change their sexual orientation and it was argued, also for various reasons, that this desire should not only be respected, but treated. Led by [Charles W.] Socarides, a psychoanalyst who, it is well-known, always disagreed with the decision to remove homosexuality from the DSM, and [Joseph] Nicolosi, a psychologist, they have described a technique known as "reparative therapy" to treat both gay men and lesbians. An organization, the National Association of Research and Therapy of Homosexuality (NARTH), was founded in 1992 and it has a newsletter, the *NARTH Bulletin*, a web site, and an annual conference. For readers interested in learning about the intellectual and ideological positions of NARTH, a subscription to the *NARTH Bulletin* is worth the few dollars it costs.

## A Heated Debate

Of course, the concept of "change" in itself is a complex parameter. Interestingly enough, the question of sexual orientation change has, over the past couple of decades, been approached from two theoretical and ideological camps that are as far apart as one can imagine. On the one hand, there is the reparative therapy movement, which is both politically and ideologically conservative and "rightist." On the other hand, there is the social constructionist movement, which is both politically and ideologically liberal and "leftist," and the constructionists, like the reparativists, have often argued that sexual orientation is more fluid than it is fixed. At times, there really is something to the expression that science and politics make strange bedfellows!

Not surprisingly, the discourse between NARTH and its critics has been extremely heated. The rhetoric about reparative therapy has far exceeded any empirical evidence about its effectiveness and efficacy, or lack thereof, and has largely focused on ethics and sexual politics. As this debate moved into formal resolutions by professional organizations critiquing "reparative therapy," it is rather disconcerting, from a (narrow) empirical perspective, that so little information is available about the outcome of this form of treatment. Such resolutions raise complex ethical issues in their own right, including matters of individual autonomy in arranging a "contractual" agreement between client and therapist. Of course, the absence of empirical information is all too common for many psychological treatments for many "problems in living" and/or disorders. In this respect, the absence of such data for "reparative therapy" is not that surprising (indeed, one might also note that, despite the multiplicity of published works on affirmative psychotherapies for gays and lesbians, they, too, lack any clear empirical foundation, at least if one uses standard guidelines for empirically-validated treatments.

## More Research Needed

It is really only in the last couple of years that we are beginning to see the semblance of some research about who exactly are the types of clients who seek out this form of treatment and some data on outcome. From a scientific standpoint, however, the empirical database remains rather primitive and any decisive claim about benefits or harms really must be taken with a rather substantial grain of salt and without such data it is difficult to understand how professional societies can issue any clear statement that is not contaminated by rhetorical fervor. Sexual science should encourage the establishment of a methodologically sound database from which more reasoned and nuanced conclusions might be drawn.

# THE BIBLE DOES NOT CONDEMN HOMOSEXUALITY

George Regas

George Regas is rector emeritus of All Saints Episcopal Church in Pasadena, California. In this selection from his *Los Angeles Times* column, he responds to a reader's bitter criticism of his support for gay marriage. He notes that many religious critics of homosexuality use biblical passages, such as the proscription against same-sex relations in Leviticus, to justify their prejudices. People who claim to interpret the Bible literally are hypocritical, says Regas, because everyone is a selective literalist. They take biblical laws against homosexuality literally while rejecting others, such as the prohibition against eating pork or the support of slavery, as antiquated and irrelevant. According to Regas, Christians who condemn gays and lesbians should reexamine the biblical portrayal of Christ's unconditional love.

I received an angry response to my recent column on gay marriage. The caller exploded with outrage that a minister of the Gospel would dare to endorse such a sinful lifestyle.

"Haven't you read about the sin of Sodom and Gomorrah? Don't you believe the Bible is the Word of God? What kind of minister are you?" She didn't allow me to answer. She hung up.

So this column must serve as my answer to this angry Christian.

Unfortunately, she is not alone. She speaks for too many religious people in this country.

## Homosexuality and the Bible

Homosexual behavior was not a big issue for the biblical writers. It is referred to only seven times in all of Scripture and nowhere in the four Gospels is it even mentioned. Not a single sentence from the lips of Jesus.

Many who condemn gay men and lesbians and want to deal with them punitively read the Bible with a selective literalism. Unquestionably, there are passages that forbid or deplore homosexual behavior, but the discussions of these texts are often superficial, if not distorted.

Take a Bible and turn to the third book which is Leviticus and read it. You will quickly understand how every religious person—fundamentalists and liberals—is selective about what is taken as God's word!

The television evangelists are always talking about the sin of Sodom and Gomorrah and how homosexuality destroyed the city. I do not know one respectable biblical scholar attributing the destruction of Sodom and Gomorrah to homosexuality. Yet the words sodomy and sodomite have come to mean the perversity of homosexuality.

As the cities of Sodom and Gomorrah were already under the sentence of doom, the destruction of Sodom could hardly have been the result of the attempted gang rape of the angels. The prophet Ezekiel makes this perfectly clear. This is how he sees it: "As surely as I live, declared the Sovereign Lord . . . now this was the sin of your sister Sodom: She and her daughters were arrogant, overfed and unconcerned; they did not help the poor and needy. They were haughty and did detestable things before me. Therefore, I did away with them as you have seen." (Ezekiel 16:48, 49)

The sin of Sodom and Gomorrah was the sin of inhospitality, the sin of hardness of heart in the presence of human need, the sin of injustice and neglecting the poor. That was the abomination to God. Those were the Sodomites. It is amazing how God's judgment upon a city for its corporate injustice has been transformed into a clarion call against private sexual behavior.

## Selective Literalism

We should be honest and give up the hypocrisy of claiming, "I am a biblical literalist," when really everyone is a selective literalist, especially those who swear by the anti-homosexual laws of the book of Leviticus and then feast on barbecued ribs and delight in watching the Super Bowl. For the literalist, the book of Leviticus says it is an abomination, not only to eat pork but merely to touch the skin of a dead pig.

If the Levitical text on homosexual behavior is made normative— "A man shall not lie with another man as with a woman"—what do we do with other prohibitions? Wearing garments made with two different materials and sowing a field with two kinds of seed?

Let's be honest about the Bible. No biblical literalist I know of still publicly advocates slavery or stoning to death an adulterer—both urged in parts of the Bible.

One day the renounced theologian, Paul Tillich, was accosted by a Bible-waving fundamentalist. "Professor Tillich, do you believe this book is the Word of God?" And the wise theologian responded, "Yes, I do if it possesses you rather than you possessing it!"

In no way do I discount the Bible. It is the foundational document, the foundation for all churches around the world. It is central to my life as a religious person. But if you take the Bible seriously, you can't read it literally and dismiss what we have learned in the centuries after the Bible was finished.

Today we know gay and lesbian couples who live deeply committed lives of love and integrity. This sexual orientation and its expression in an honorable relationship was not the subject matter of the biblical writers. The really serious problem for Christians who live by "The Book" is not how to square homosexuality with certain passages which on the surface condemn it—but rather how to reconcile rejection, prejudice and cruelty toward gays with the gracious, unconditional love of Christ.

In any event, I read something of [peace activist] William Sloan Coffin that still haunts me. In a Washington cemetery on the gravestone of a Vietnam veteran, it is written: "When I was in the military, they gave me a medal for killing two men and discharged me for loving one."

# THE BIBLE CONDEMNS HOMOSEXUALITY

Wisconsin Christians United

The organization Wisconsin Christians United (WCU) states that its primary mission is to educate people about the sin of homosexuality and the agenda of the homosexual movement. In the following selection the WCU argues that many scriptures in the Bible clearly and repeatedly denounce all homosexual acts. Because God condemns sexual acts other than those between married, heterosexual couples, says the WCU, homosexual acts must be outlawed. If people capitulate to homosexuals in the name of "tolerance" and "diversity," they put themselves and society in danger of being severely judged by God.

The Bible, Old Testament and New, has much to say about homosexual acts such as sodomy. The Bible is clear that God has declared such acts to be sin. For instance, God calls the homosexual acts committed by the men of Sodom "very grievous" (Gen. 18:20). He also calls those perverse sexual acts "filthy," "wicked," "ungodly," and "unlawful" (II Peter 2:6–8). In the book of Jude, verse 7, God explains that the inhabitants of Sodom and Gomorrah were destroyed for "fornication" with "strange flesh." In this, God contrasts homosexual sex acts with sexual relations between one man and one woman in His created, holy institution of marriage where the two become "one flesh" (Gen. 2:24). God has forbidden and cursed all fornication, the joining of human beings as "one flesh" in a sexual union outside of marriage (I Cor. 6:9–11). In I Corinthians 6:15–20, He condemns the sexual acts men commit with women prostitutes because the two become "one flesh" outside of marriage. Homosexual acts are especially evil in that they are "fornication . . . [with] strange flesh."

Throughout the Holy Scriptures, the homosexual wickedness of Sodom is referred to and used as a sort of benchmark for evil. Of course, because the Scriptures use the phrase to know when speaking of that famous incident when a crowd of sodomites demanded to have sex with two men visitors staying in Sodom, some have tried to say the sodomites only wanted to get acquainted with those visitors, who were in reality angels! This is ridiculously poor biblical scholarship. The Hebrew verb *yada*, which translates to the English verb to know is used in several scriptural contexts, including to denote sexual intercourse as in Genesis 4:1: "And Adam knew Eve his wife; and she conceived, and bare Cain. . . ." No, the sodomites attempting to break down Lot's door did not simply want to shake hands with his visitors! That is as foolish as saying that Sodom was destroyed because its inhabitants did not care for the poor! That particular claim is founded in a distortion of Ezekiel 16:48–50. In this biblical passage, God's people were being warned that they were acting worse than the people of Sodom had by the very fact that they were God's chosen people and yet were committing abominable sins! The verses contain a short chronological account of how the citizens of Sodom, which was located in a "well watered" area, became lazy and selfish in prosperity. Eventually, they also became "haughty" and committed "abomination," a reference to sodomy and other homosexual acts. At that point, God judged and destroyed the town. Yes, the citizens of Sodom were selfish, and that was wrong. However, Sodom was clearly destroyed by God because it had become a sodomite culture.

Still, some pro-homosexual champions claim the Bible does not condemn homosexual acts. Yet, it does so from cover to cover. The Bible condemns homosexual acts in the strongest of terms and even by describing the acts themselves, such as in Leviticus 18:22: "Thou shalt not lie with mankind, as with womankind: it is abomination." Leviticus 18:22 and Leviticus 20:13 both graphically forbid sexual acts between two men. Romans 1:26 forbids sexual acts between two women, labeling "lesbianism" unnatural, saying that women who do those things "change" the natural for that which is "against nature." So much for the "born that way" argument. Romans 1:27 condemns sexual acts between men and men. Verse twenty-seven begins with "And likewise also the men. . . ." I Corinthians 6:9–11 is a warning against the deception that one can live in open rebellion to God's law and still be a Christian headed for heaven. In that passage, sodomites are accurately and plainly called "abusers of themselves with mankind." I Timothy 1:8–11 instructs on the lawful use of the law to punish persons who commit acts such as murder, perjury, and sodomy. Here homosexuals are graphically described as "them that defile themselves with mankind." Both of those descriptive phrases, like all New Testament references to those guilty of committing sodomy, are faithfully translated from the word *arsenokoites*, the Greek word which describes homosexual sex acts. Greek was the language in which the New Testament was originally written. Of course, until recent times, no one attempted to claim that the Bible does not condemn and outlaw homosexual sex. That may be in part because one must play the part of a fool to do so (Rom. 1:22).

# Misguided Justifications of Homosexuality

Consider for a moment a few more of the desperate excuses which have been concocted of late to justify sodomy and other homosexual acts. There are some who smugly overlook all the biblical condemnations and prohibitions of homosexual acts other than those occurring in the book of Leviticus where those acts are called "abomination." They then state, "So what if God calls homosexual acts an abomination in the Bible; He also calls the eating of shellfish an 'abomination.'" Of course, these people may or may not realize that the ban on eating of shellfish was part of the Mosaic dietary law which was set aside by God when Jesus Christ instituted a new covenant through His shed blood (Luke 22:20). They also may be ignorant of the fact that the word rendered abomination in the Old Testament comes from six different closely related Hebrew words. When the Bible says that eating shellfish is an abomination under the Mosaic dietary rules, abomination in that case is rendered from the Hebrew word *sheqets*, which means filthy. Under the Mosaic dietary laws, the Hebrews were to consider shellfish filthy, that is unclean, food. On the other hand, the Hebrew word which describes homosexual acts is *toebah*. *Vine's Complete Expository Dictionary of Old and New Testament Words* (c.1984) accurately states that *toebah* ". . . defines something or someone as essentially unique in the sense of being 'dangerous,' 'sinister,' and 'repulsive.'. . ." The Bible tells us that God judges sodomy to be *toebah*.

When it comes to those two verses in the book of Leviticus which condemn men sodomizing each other, there are some homosexual apologists who disingenuously state that those verses only condemn "cultic sexual acts between men" but that those verses do not condemn "loving gay relationships." That particular argument goes up in smoke rather quickly in light of the rest of the Bible and also when one considers that the Leviticus prohibitions on homosexual acts are smack dab in the middle of prohibitions on other perverted sexual behavior such as bestiality and incest. If God is only condemning "cultic homosexual acts" in the Leviticus passages, then it would follow that He is also only condemning "cultic sex with animals" and "cultic incest." Of course, there is no such thing as legitimate sexual relations between a person and an animal or between a parent and a child anymore than sexual relations between man and man or woman and woman are legitimate. God, in His Word, condemns all sexual activity other than that between a man and a woman in the holy estate of matrimony.

As already noted, God's Word is crystal clear and extremely strong in the condemnation of homosexual acts. In Judges 19:22, homosexuals are referred to as "sons of Belial"; and in Judges 20:13, they are called "children of Belial." The word *Belial* denotes individuals who are ungodly and wicked. That is exactly how God views those who engage in homosexual acts.

So it is true; from cover to cover, the Word of God condemns homosexual acts such as sodomy. This should not be surprising since those acts are a complete repudiation of God's created order and represent a graphic rebellion against the Creator and Lawgiver of the universe. Homosexual acts go even beyond the sin which "is common to man" (I Cor. 10:13) and launch off into sin which is "unnatural" (Rom. 1:26–27). Consequently, homosexual acts are incredibly destructive to the individual who commits them (Rom. 1:27–28, Gal. 6:7) and to the nation which allows and condones them. With regard to the latter, God's Word has made it clear He will judge and destroy a nation which allows homosexual acts.

It may be popular in today's culture to defend and promote sexual perversion in the name of "tolerance" and "diversity"; but the truth is, God hates such acts and judges them severely. Homosexuals do not need, and must not be given, encouragement to continue in their destructive, sinful behavior. In accordance with the "Laws of Nature's God" (Declaration of Independence), homosexuals acts must be re-criminalized by the civil government (I Tim. 1:8–11, Rom. 13:4). Upholding true law in such a way is also showing true love. Ecclesiastes 8:11: "Because sentence against an evil work is not executed speedily, therefore the heart of the sons of men is fully set in them to do evil." Homosexuals should be told that they, as all sinners, are lost and headed for hell unless they repent, believe in the Lord Jesus Christ, and are saved (Rom. 10:13). Christians must stand against the New Sodom which has sprung up in our midst. At the same time, we must share the gospel with the sodomites and pray that some will be born again and justified by faith in Jesus Christ (Jn. 3:3, I Cor. 6:11). Now you know what God's revealed Word, the Bible, says about homosexual acts. For your own sake, I hope that you will not try to change the meaning of His words or add to them. Proverbs 30:6: "Add thou not unto his words, lest he reprove thee, and thou be found a liar."

# GAY ISSUES SHOULD BE TAUGHT IN SCHOOL

Kevin Jennings

Kevin Jennings believes that the campaigns to ban any representation of gay issues in schools play on parents' fears that homosexuals recruit children. Some of the people who lead these campaigns claim that they want to ensure that parents have control over what their children learn, but in reality they want the power to indoctrinate students in what they consider to be American values. For Jennings, good education is not about turning out like-minded automatons but about teaching children critical thinking so they can evaluate ideas and develop their intellectual abilities. The study of homosexuality, like any school topic, can provide a valuable opportunity for students to openly discuss a controversial subject, share ideas and viewpoints, and think for themselves. Jennings is the founder and executive director of the Gay, Lesbian, and Straight Education Network (GLSEN), an organization that works to meet the needs of lesbian, gay, bisexual, and transgender students and teachers.

The Radical Right is increasingly targeting gays in general, and gay issues in education in particular, as part of an overall strategy to impose their vision of America on the rest of the country. They have been able to play on the fears of many well-meaning people to advance this agenda. The basic worry of every parent is, "Is my kid safe?" By playing on the myth that homosexuals recruit children, reactionary attacks on inclusive education direct a positive impulse— the desire to have the best for one's children—toward a destructive end—intolerance for others.

This became poignantly clear to me when I traveled to Merrimack, New Hampshire in August [1999]. Townspeople in Merrimack were fighting an anti-gay policy being put forth by some reactionary board members, a policy that would ban any representation of gay issues in a positive or even a neutral light. At the request of local organizers, I came to Merrimack to speak at a rally being held the night the school board was set to vote on the policy.

I arrived early so I could observe the school board debate. Perhaps because I was wearing a tie, a mother in her mid-thirties standing near me decided I must be on her side of an argument that had divided the large audience in attendance, the bulk of whom seemed to be against the policy's passage. She sidled over to me and began to unload her frustration with what she saw as a foreign issue that had no place in her town's schools. Saying all she wanted was "pure education" for her children, she finally exploded. "What does homosexuality have to do with education?" she demanded. . . .

## Critical Thinking Is the Heart of Good Education

To answer her question, we have to first answer another: What is a good education? For me, education is about learning to think. A good teacher is one that takes a subject that matters to his or her students and helps them to think about it in a thoughtful, critical manner. In America, we have also traditionally seen the opportunity to get an education as the first step on the road to success, and created the world's first free public school system to make sure that all people got an equal chance to develop the critical faculties that are the product of a good education. Good public education is an essential part of a democracy where the citizens rule and are free to advance themselves as far as their abilities, ambitions and hard work will take them.

Homosexuality itself has nothing to do with education, any more than biology, chemistry, algebra or any other subject does. What is important is what one can learn from the study of a given subject. A discussion of how we understand homosexuality in our culture and how this reflects our values, beliefs and world view has tremendous educational value. It is clearly a subject that matters to kids: they talk about it, they ask about it, they use phrases like "That's so gay" routinely, so few can argue that it isn't a subject that needs addressing (although some will, believe me!). The question is, can we use it to help students think and learn? The answer is manifestly yes.

## Teaching American Values

But this is not the agenda of folks who put forth policies like that passed in Merrimack on August 14. They see education serving a different purpose. For them, schools are there to inculcate values: developing independent thought is not the overriding goal. And they call upon a strong historic tradition in this belief. The vast growth of public education in late nineteenth century America was fueled, at least in part, by the fears of native whites who saw the influx of southern and eastern European immigrants as a threat to their way of life. They saw the public schools as means to "Americanize" these foreign elements and to indoctrinate them with "American values."

Today, many families feel bewildered by the rapid cultural change sweeping our nation, and some have been led to believe that a "gay agenda" is, at least in part, responsible for what they see as a breakdown of our society and a seemingly bleak future for their children. They feel that if they can regain some sense of control over what goes on in their community's schools, maybe the whole society will become a little more coherent. They often just want to feel as if things are not completely out of control. So they come out to public meetings and demand to know what homosexuality has to do with education, and demand that it be banished so that the schools can return to the basics of reading, 'riting and 'rithmetic.

## Parental Control

Sadly these people are pawns in a game, a game wherein unscrupulous politicos manipulate their very real and legitimate concerns for short-term political gain. Those doing the manipulating cleverly fly the banner of "parental control." They protest that they have nothing against gays—Merrimack school board members who voted for the policy in question repeatedly said they were not prejudiced and would not tolerate verbal gay-bashing in their schools—but that they only wish to make sure that parents have the final say over what their children learn. Who could be against that?

It will do no good to point out the illogic of this position. Parents have little say over the day-to-day teachings of a school, and any school where they did would quickly become an unmanageable bureaucratic nightmare. Imagine if every lesson plan had to be approved by parents before implemented—nothing would get taught at all while we attended interminable board hearings. Parental control is only invoked when a particular subset of parents wants to impose their own values on a school.

Pointing this out, however, would have lad little effect on the mother with whom I spoke in Merrimack. She had real fears about her children, and wanted them addressed. Knowing this, we must start thinking now about how to speak to her fears. We must help her understand that an education that teaches her children to think for themselves, rather than one that turns them into automatons, is her best hope for securing their future in the global marketplace. We must help her understand that bigotry and name-calling represent a greater threat to her child's welfare than an open discussion of touchy issues. . . .

In short, we must help her understand that homosexuality is not a threat to her children: homophobia is.

That is what homosexuality has do to with education. It's about freedom of thought, it's about the ability to use one's mind, it's about the right to be educated rather than trained. And we have to help people who don't understand that to get it.

# GAY ISSUES SHOULD NOT BE TAUGHT IN SCHOOL

Jeff Cullers

Teaching lessons in school that present gay and lesbian relation-ships as normal or positive, argues Jeff Cullers, seriously tres-passes on the rights of schoolchildren and their parents. In this selection Cullers criticizes diversity programs like those recom-mended by the Gay, Lesbian, and Straight Education Network for two reasons. First, he argues that public schools do not have the right to try to teach students to accept homosexuality because such moral education is the responsibility of parents. Second, he finds it intolerable that gay and lesbian rights activists target ele-mentary schoolchildren, an audience that has little capacity to understand and critically evaluate sexuality issues. At the time he wrote this selection, Cullers was a student at Carnegie Mellon University and the photo editor of the student-run *Tartan* news-paper, in which this essay appeared.

Most parents agree that when they send their children to public school, they should return home with the same set of values. The pur-pose of public school is to teach, not embark on a crusade of social conditioning. However, the gay agenda sees it differently. "Children should be a special target for homosexual rights activists in the attempt to change society," said Urvashi Vaid, former executive direc-tor of the National Gay and Lesbian Task Force, at a press conference.

Such is the goal for gay activists—to change American society by imposing their beliefs on people. Tolerance for the gay lifestyle is not enough. By "tolerance" I mean not interfering in someone's beliefs or activities even though one may not agree. In the eyes of the gay agenda, American society must not only tolerate the gay lifestyle, but be convinced that such a lifestyle is perfectly normal. Never mind the fact that the precious moral and religious beliefs of millions of Ameri-cans are being trampled. Most people who have an established moral or religious opposition to homosexuality can filter out or ignore

Jeff Cullers, "Gay Agenda Goes Too Far," *The Tartan*, September 16, 2002. Copyright © 2002 by Jeff Cullers. Reproduced by permission.

homosexual propaganda, compelling gay activists to take up their cause in public schools.

## Conversion Through Curriculum

Their method involves infiltrating public schools behind the facade of diversity appreciation. By far the guiltiest organization involved in the practice of homosexual brainwashing of children is the Gay Lesbian Straight Education Network. As stated on their website, GLSEN "envisions a future in which every child learns to respect and accept all people, regardless of sexual orientation or gender identity/expression," ostensibly to help make schools "safe" for homosexuals. What GLSEN ignores is the fine line between respect and conversion.

Based on its activities, it is obvious that GLSEN's goal is convincing school children that being gay is okay. Thus far confined to a few liberal states, GLSEN discusses and even demonstrates graphic homosexual activities to students as early as the eighth grade. At GLSEN conferences, teachers are taught how to incorporate discussions of homosexuality into their class time. They are given videos for their students that portray homosexual couples as being in completely normal, everyday relationships. Activists are invited to elementary schools (that would be 5–12-year-olds) to hold assemblies in which they teach kids about all kinds of families, but somehow neglect to mention the true family of a husband and wife. GLSEN has even been talking to Nickelodeon to spread their ideology with a pro-homosexual cartoon.

These activities are sickening and wrong on many fronts. First, public schools have no right or duty to tamper with the moral state of their students. Bringing up homosexuality might be permissible for older, middle school children, but only in a non-biased way that is lost to most activists. Currently activists are getting to elementary kids before parents even talk to them about normal sexuality, and that is a problem. To many people, sexuality IS a profoundly moral issue, not some mere "lifestyle choice." Schools are not authorized to introduce and take sides on such an issue. "It is imperative to begin addressing these issues in the elementary schools as early as possible," says Stephen Hicks of GLSEN-Los Angeles. I don't think so; what right does this person have to go over parents' heads and speak to elementary kids about these "issues?"

## Targeting Children

A second reason to get the gay agenda out of school is that the target audience (children) of GLSEN's efforts probably does not have the capacity to truly comprehend the message. Unfortunately, this works to GLSEN's advantage, since elementary students who do not have the intellectual development to grasp any type of sexuality will be more accepting. How can you argue that kids understand the message when five-year-old girls are asking: "Daddy, I don't like boys; does this mean

I am a lesbian?" I did not know five-year-olds used seven-syllable words like "homosexuality."

The most compelling reason against homosexual indoctrination in schools is that the right of parents to raise their children with the values they see fit is being violated. Schools should not push any moral issues, such as homosexuality, on their students. This is why parents have the right to opt their kids out of sex ed. The whole purpose of doing so is defeated, though, if teachers decide to randomly introduce homosex ed, or hold "sexual diversity appreciation" assemblies. I don't want to know the details of a homosexual relationship, and I certainly would not want my child in middle school learning about it, or my second grader coming home saying that the rhyme of the day was "I'm gay and that's okay." This actually happened in California! In my opinion, being gay is not okay and no one has any business convincing my child otherwise, but my beliefs do not mean I am going to start some kind of hate group.

Obviously GLSEN is not the only entity leading the charge to morally alter children for its own purposes. Numerous groups want to change America in the same way. National Educators Association President Bob Chase has officially endorsed the disgusting idea of fostering gay activism in schools. The gay agenda seeks to have its constituency treated as an underrepresented minority, complete with special rights and "diversity asset" status. The big problem is that not many people believe it is wrong to be a minority, while an awful lot of people believe it is indeed wrong to be gay. Disagreeing with homosexuality is a moral and, for many, a religious judgment on homosexual behavior and does not represent a threat to homosexuals if such disapproval is accompanied by tolerance. Similarly, I may not approve of drivers who turn their car stereos all the way up, but I am going to tolerate it without any problem. Unfortunately, current efforts to infiltrate public schools demonstrate that such a peaceful arrangement is inadequate for the gay agenda.

# CHAPTER 5

# GAYS AND LESBIANS: PERSONAL NARRATIVES

Contemporary Issues
Companion

# My Life as an Asian American Queer Activist in High School

Pabitra Benjamin

As a young, gay Asian American immigrant, Pabitra Benjamin has lived in many different communities that have played a part in shaping her identity. In this selection she describes her life in her home country of Nepal, in American schools, and in her multiracial family. She also discusses her life as an activist fighting against racism and homophobia. Her experiences have taught her that schools, and especially teachers, can help students learn to celebrate diversity if they have the training and resources to address intolerance when it shows up in the classroom. She argues that schools and parents need to allow young people room to discuss and explore issues such as homosexuality in order to help them develop into independent and self-confident citizens.

Sophomore year is when I really started identifying myself as queer or bi and associating with that part of the school community. Looking back on it, throughout my childhood, I had always known that I had feelings that differed from the norm, but I never knew what it was because it was never apparent. There wasn't the choice to be gay.

A year earlier, during my first year in high school, one of my mom's friends, who is gay, said, "I think your daughter's gay." My mom said, "No, no, no," and later came up to me and asked me. I answered, "Of course not." But that same year I started making friends with seniors, the "weird" ones who were gay or experimenting. They made me think and question myself. Sophomore year I met more people, and I made friends who were very open about differences. I ended up falling deeply for some females, and that's when I came out. In my junior year I ended up falling for my current girlfriend. I didn't get her until a year later, but I got her!

## Family Matters

The hardest thing about being queer is that my mom doesn't know. As in "traditional" Nepali culture, she wants grandchildren and she wants a son-in-law and she wants a "normal" life. If I told her I was gay, it would threaten this dream that she's always had. It's possible that she could respond positively and say, "Great, I knew, I'm glad you told me, you can still have kids and you can adapt." But more likely I think she'd freak out. She would never kick me out, she'd never disown me, but we would have a lot of tension for a while. And eventually she may come about but it's just not something that I'm ready to deal with right now.

I told my dad in the beginning of this year. Nowadays, he doesn't care. My girlfriend sleeps over and he's very comfortable with that, in contrast to my mom who keeps asking why I'm with my girlfriend so often. But my dad wasn't always that comfortable. Early on, we had a long discussion, an hours-long discussion about it. He has always been a very open-minded man and he just said that he would start talking about it more in order to get rid of his own homophobia. As for my mom, my dad and I talked about whether or not we should tell her, and decided not to, at least not yet. My brother knows about it and he's comfortable with it. I had told my brother before I told my father. Actually, my brother kept it a secret for two years, which is amazing because he's a little boy (he's eleven now).

It's interesting that my dad's been so open because of the fact that, or perhaps despite the fact that, for him, fighting homophobia is not a big fight. He once told me, "I don't think it's a fight. It's not as important to me as oppression in third-world countries." But it is! Our lives have been quite different. My dad's American. My birth father died when I was young, so my dad married my mom when I was three or four, and has been my dad since. He's from Chicago, but lived in Nepal half his life, doing his PhD and master's there.

I also have moved around quite a bit. I've lived in four different states, two different countries. As a result, I've had many different types of friends. When I lived in Nepal, my closest friends were from all over the world because I went to an international school. Then I came to Wisconsin, to a place where everybody was just white, and it was hard adjusting. It was difficult trying to find myself when everyone around me was white and when I was not only one of the only students of color, but also one who was able to acknowledge this racial difference. On top of that, there's the fact that I lived a very out lifestyle. Some of the worst memories I have were of trying to fit, to be accepted with all of my identities. If I were in Nepal, it would be even more so the case that I can't be out as gay or bi. In Nepal, our family's not like American Nepalis. They're Nepali Nepali. They're middle class, live in small apartments, and don't speak very much English. Their ideas are very "traditional," so it would be difficult. Similarly, if I lived in a queer community in the United States, I don't know if I'd be accepted as Asian. I wish I could live in a world where I could just be all of it at once.

## Activism

Changing communities has been the focus of my activism since the beginning of high school. Over the past few years, I've been involved in about twenty-five groups. I led about six of them, and actually started three of them. What prompted my involvement in all these groups was my earlier experience in a group called Bridges. The purpose of Bridges was to unite people, and we worked mostly on racial harmony and racial understanding. We took an approach to racial harmony that did not simply acknowledge that, "Okay, there's a lot of racism" but actually examined racism and brought difficult topics out in the open. After Bridges, in ninth and tenth grades, I continued to involve myself in work that dealt with race relations. More recently, in my junior and senior years, I've been doing work that deals more specifically with sexuality and homophobia.

I think racism and homophobia are part of the same fight. But I know many people don't agree. I see a lot of anger coming from both communities. I hear African Americans or Asian Americans say, "Oh, well, they're gay and they're the ones that reinforce that stereotype of gay people." Similarly, I hear GLBT [gay, lesbian, bisexual and transgendered] people say, "Oh wow, they're enforcing the stereotype of us and we don't like that, and they're really mean," as was the case in response to Ron Greer, a black minister who led anti-GLBT efforts in Wisconsin recently. There's just a lot of bitterness. Sometimes different communities of color fight each other rather than joining to fight racism. African Americans and Asian Americans often don't get along here. I think many African Americans think that Asian Americans are making a lot of money. It's a stereotype that isn't always true, but they sometimes focus on how Asians own the grocery stores and are taking the money of the African-American communities who live nearby. The two groups are forced by society to mix together in ways that end up separating them. I wish there was a way that we could just unite instead of having to fight about little differences.

## Celebrating Diversity

Since my first year in high school, one of my main goals has been to have some sort of day when everybody could get together to celebrate our differences and the diversity among us. Last year, we started a Diversity Day where we had booths set up by different student groups. This year, we had three days of Diversity Days. The first day we had speakers and performances. The second day we had panels all day long. The third day we had a potluck. The events were small but very effective. My goal over these past two years was to keep it continuing and to involve more of the school and not just a few classes in the celebration. This year, out of a population of 2,000 students, at least 500 or 600 took part. That was one of my largest accomplishments.

Another big accomplishment was my school's GSA [gay-straight alliance]. In my junior year, I helped start a gay-straight alliance with three senior friends. This year, since all three friends had graduated, I took over the leadership of the GSA, and we became one of the largest clubs at my high school. We had about thirty members, with around fifteen people coming to the weekly meetings. Most of them were straight, though we never asked about anyone's sexual orientation, especially since some had not yet decided. The group provided both a supportive space and a means for activism. For example, at the beginning of the year, we decided that one of our main goals would be to stop students from using the word "gay" as a form of verbal bashing. It was extremely commonplace to hear "That's so gay" or "He's such a fag." By the end of the year, the use of such language had noticeably decreased. We even heard people whom we previously thought to be homophobic say things like, "You know what, I don't like the use of that language." It was exciting to think that, by going out and standing strong, we started that. We were on a mission, and through personal contacts, got more and more people to help spread that knowledge.

This is one of the most important areas where teachers need to do more. They need to acknowledge that gay-bashing happens, that little things like name-calling are part of a bigger circle of homophobia that permeates schools. If teachers heard the word "nigger," they would automatically jump, but if they hear the word "gay," they often let it go instead of stopping and saying, "You know, let's talk about this." And I don't mean that teachers should merely say, "No, that's wrong, don't use that word." They need to stop class and have a discussion. It might take only five minutes, but they need to say, "Let's talk about this."

In fact, teachers need to be prepared to talk about any sort of subject that comes up—sexism, racism, homophobia, anything. I think that that is the most important thing for which teachers need preparation. The leaders of the local school board recently called me. They're planning a workshop for the entire school board on how to deal with GLBTQ [gay, lesbian, bisexual, transgendered, and queer] students. I'm going to be involved in that workshop. More opportunities are needed to take steps like that to educate members of the school board who can then educate teachers. Teachers and students need to talk. There needs to be a day on which teachers could have an in-service workshop, not about graduation tests, but about what it's like for GLBTQ high school students. That would be a major help.

## Living with Homophobia

There was a time when I was sitting on a school lawn with my girlfriend, just sitting there like two friends, tickling, whatever. All of a sudden this guy comes up to her and says, "Why don't you just stop that 'cause that's nasty. I mean you guys just look . . ." And I said, "What? You know what, if you could ask a little bit nicer, I would stop, even though I don't know what I'm doing wrong." We got in this huge fight and he said, "Come on, bitch, come hit me." And I said, "What are you talking about?" There were around seventeen or eighteen people out there. I asked, "Who here thinks this guy is wrong?" Everybody raised their hands, including his friends. It may have been wrong for me to isolate him, but that's the way I do things; I'm very blunt. I wanted him to know that he was wrong.

This is the kind of environment that exists in schools. And what happens in school affects our experiences elsewhere because people gossip and talk. Gay couples can be conversation topics for many other people. My girlfriend's mom is a teacher, and the news that we were going out had spread from a far-west-side high school to a far-east-side elementary school. Thankfully, she already knew. But we were teachers' gossip for a while. And that's probably the hardest part of high school life. I don't ever know what people are really thinking. I'm not saying that people ever understand who they are but high school can be a pretty confusing time without this added problem. The secrecy often surrounding homophobia impacts all of our lives.

Fortunately, my family upbringing prepared me to live with independence and self-confidence. My family and I have lived all sorts of lifestyles. We have traveled and lived in many places because my dad gets jobs here and gets fired there. With all these changes, my parents are used to giving me lots of freedom. It's as if they say, "Just go on, do whatever you want. We're not going to keep an eye out every minute." They trust me. They didn't know about all of my extracurricular activities until I started winning awards. Even now, they don't know about half of what I do, but they know I do things and are okay with that. If I come home at three in the morning, they do ask, "Why are you late?" but if I simply say, "I was with a friend doing this," they trust me. That trust and ability to just go and do whatever I wanted to do helped me become an activist. It helped me see the kind of changes I wanted to make. It did not lead to what parents often fear, namely, that "Oh, if I give my kids freedom, they're going to go and do drugs and everything, go get in trouble." Yes, I've done drugs and things like that, but that's been a part of my growing-up experiences. And being allowed to try different things is important.

I think the most important advice I can give to anybody is what I said about my parents: Parents need to let their children go. Not all kids will do good things. But parents need to accept the ways their children are different, be they GLBT or simply choosing to do some things and not following the paths of others. Parents need to talk to their kids, know how to help them, and even define some boundaries together, but let them be on their own. I can't give advice about how to stop racism or how to stop homophobia, but I can say that a lot more youths are coming out these days. If you have a friend whose child is GLBT, be willing to go up to that child or your friend, or anyone, and just talk to them about it. Talk to your friends about how it's okay.

# I Am a Gay Orthodox Rabbi

Steve Greenberg

For many years Steve Greenberg felt that two parts of his identity—being both Jewish and gay—were incompatible. As a teenager he went against the wishes of his family to choose the life of an Orthodox Jew. However, his calling was increasingly threatened by his attraction to boys while attending yeshiva school because same-sex desire was clearly forbidden by the sacred Torah. The clashing elements of his identity made him feel like an outsider in his synagogue. In this selection Greenberg narrates the difficult journey he undertook to integrate the two seemingly irreconcilable parts of his life. As the first openly gay Orthodox rabbi, he helped to found a new gay and lesbian community center in Jerusalem.

I am a gay Orthodox rabbi. I resisted this identity for a long time. Throughout the years when I struggled with it, many would counsel me to reject one or the other of these inert elements. An Orthodox friend urged me not to barter my soul for sexual freedom. Gay friends told me to get out of the Orthodox world, which they saw as intractable, cruel, and oppressive. Sometimes I wondered if I was fooling myself to think that with enough effort, oxygen and hydrogen might be squeezed into water. Thankfully, there were moments when a glimmer of possibility shone through, when I could begin to see how the Torah might be read differently, how Talmudic passages could add up in other than damning ways. It took me five years to do the research for a book that argues just this, that gay Orthodox Jews are neither wanton sinners nor obsessive compulsives for seeking both the intimate love of partner and the love of God. The intellectual and religious justification was just the last act of the story. The two journeys, religious and sexual, while not simultaneous, are intertwined over a period of almost twenty years. Becoming a gay Orthodox rabbi has taken more than half my life.

The Orthodox story is easier to plot. I adopted traditional Jewish observance in my teens. An Orthodox rabbi had introduced me to the vertical and horizontal Jewish worlds. What I call the vertical world is the world of intellect and meaning. Studying Talmud felt like a feast

Steve Greenberg, "A Gay Orthodox Rabbi," *Queer Jews*, edited by David Shneer and Caryn Aviv. New York: Routledge, 2002. Copyright © 2002 by Routledge/Taylor & Francis Books, Inc. Reproduced by permission of the publisher and the author.

of the mind with scholars of six different centuries invited to share in the conversation. The horizontal world was the world shaped by the people of the little Orthodox community that welcomed me in. Overcoming my parents' resistance, I excitedly escaped Columbus, Ohio, to attend Yeshiva University in New York City.

Becoming Orthodox was a spiritual and intellectual conversion accomplished over two years. Despite the conflict between my gay life and my Orthodox Jewish life trajectories, most of the important coming-out episodes of my life were within the embrace of my new-found Orthodox community. The stories below come together, to mark a set of passages. The genesis of my gay identity begins with a childhood seder [Passover ceremonial dinner].

## Passover 1966

In my youth, we attended the seders of my mother's elder cousin, a survivor of Bergen-Belsen [concentration camp] whom we affectionately called Uncle Al. Al had a gentle high-pitched voice peppered with a raspy Yiddish accent. His singsong chant of the Haggadah was done without much attention to the written text. He had learned the Haggadah *baal-pe*, by heart, sometime after a number was burned into his skin. In the camps where forgetfulness was blessing, only those things burned into memory or onto flesh remained. Aunt Charlotte had married my Uncle Al after a divorce. She and Uncle Al raised her two children, but had none of their own.

Those seders were of course occasions of great excitement for us children. Lots of unusual relatives that we saw only on Pesach [Passover], joined to my family by this single cousin of my mother, sat around an endless table, anxious and ready for the festivities to begin. Aunt Charlotte shuttled back and forth from the dining room to the huge kitchen, which, by seder time, was bursting with incredible quantities of unbelievably delicious glatt kosher food. While the kitchen always seemed ready to explode, the dining room was always more patient. Not so attentive, but respectful, guests were annually washed in the eerie angelic drone of Uncle Al's recitation of the Haggadah, as if in Bergen-Belsen with his eyes closed.

An unspoken honor was given to this hardened man with a high-pitched voice. Never was a word uttered to anyone about what happened to him during the war. Charlotte protected him from the nightmares and migraines he would experience if he dared to talk about those times. Surrounded by his wife's family, there was a quiet sadness about him. While the noise and activity rose and fell throughout the seder, Al held court at two seders, separated by his weighted brow and joined by his high-pitched *galitsianer* Yiddish singsong.

Every year, Aunt Charlotte's sister brought her two kids. Jackie and Terry were late teens during my early adolescence and they were both stunningly beautiful. Only years later in recounting the occasions of those seders did my mother bring back the memory of those two beautiful youths.

On a visit home to Columbus, Ohio, we sat around and reminisced about those wonderful seders. At some point in the stories, my mother interjected that Marc, my younger brother by three years, could not keep his eyes off of Jackie. She had remembered with a glint, a motherly smile, that her son of nine or ten years had an obvious crush on Jackie, the teenage beauty. What she did not notice, and what I did not remember until that very moment, was that I was transfixed every year by Terry. The conscious memories of Uncle Al and Aunt Charlotte, the smells, the tastes, the sounds of Uncle Al's high-pitched chanting had all along protected a dangerous and exciting secret. I looked forward to those seders every year, in no small measure, to feast my eyes on Terry's dark eyes, his fluid manner, his dimpled smile. No one at the table could have noticed how I spent half the night staring at him. Terry's specific presence in my mind was covered by the absence of a category in which to place him. Instead, the erotics of his presence simply mixed in with everything like a fragrant spice.

A few years later, the arrival of the hormonal hurricane left me completely dumbfounded. Just when my body should have fulfilled social expectations, it began to transgress them. I had no physical response to girls. When other boys became enraptured by girls, I found my rapture in learning Torah. I was thrilled by the sprawling rabbinic arguments, the imaginative plays on words, and the demand for meaning everywhere. *Negiah*, the prohibition to embrace, kiss, or even touch girls until marriage, was my saving grace. The premarital sexual restraint of the tradition was a perfect mask, not only to the world, but to myself.

## Yeshiva Life

My years in yeshiva were spectacular, in some measure because they were so intensely fueled by a totally denied sexuality. There were many *bachurim* (students) in the yeshiva whose intense and passionate learning was energized with repressed sexual energy. For me, the environment deflected sexual energy and generated it as well. The male spirit and energy I felt in yeshiva was both nourishing and frustrating. I do not know if I was alone among my companions or not. From those early years, I remember no signs by which I could have clearly read my gayness or anyone else's. I only know that I was plagued with stomach aches almost every morning.

In 1976, beset with an increased awareness of my attraction to a fellow yeshiva student, I visited a sage, Rav Eliashuv, who lives in one of the most secluded right-wing Orthodox communities in Jerusalem. He was old and in failing health, but still taking visitors who daily waited in an anteroom for hours for the privilege of speaking with him for a few minutes. Speaking in Hebrew, I told him what, at the time, I felt was the truth: "Master, I am attracted to both men and women. What shall I do?" He responded, "My dear one, my friend, then you have twice the power of love. Use it carefully." I was stunned. I sat in silence for a moment, waiting for more. "Is that all?" I asked. He smiled and said, "That is all. There is nothing more to say."

Rav Eliashuv's words calmed me, permitting me to forget temporarily the awful tensions that would eventually overtake me. His trust and support buoyed me above my fears. I thought that as a bisexual I could have a wider and richer emotional life and perhaps even a deeper spiritual life than is common—and still marry and have a family.

For a long while I felt a self-acceptance that carried me confidently into rabbinical school. I began rabbinical training with great excitement and a sense of promise. At the center of my motivations were those powerful rabbinic traditions that had bowled me over in my early adolescence. I wanted more than anything else to learn and to teach Torah in its full depth and breadth. I finished rabbinical school, still dating women and carefully avoiding any physical expression, and took my first jobs as a rabbi. There were many failed relationships with wonderful women who could not understand why things just didn't work out.

## Exploring the Gay Community

Ten years after the encounter with Rabbi Eliashuv, in 1986, I was living in New York City and finally trying to make sense of my life. I decided to enter the Gay and Lesbian Community Center on Thirteenth Street in Manhattan. I had passed it many times without going in. I wondered if I should take my kippah [head cover] off or not. Eventually I went inside, head uncovered. There was a meeting of Act Up inside, boisterous and blatant. I sat at the back wondering if I belonged here. I wandered to the bulletin board later and stumbled across a young man, perhaps in his late twenties, in a streimel [round hat] and long black coat, white knickers, and earlocks. I was in shock: "What is a Satmar Hasid [traditional Hasidic Jew] doing here?"

Barely able to open my mouth, not knowing quite what to say, I asked him, "Are you . . . ?" He replied, "Yeah, I am gay." At that moment, a million thoughts flooded my mind. What an amazing capacity to wander into this place, looking like he does. What does he do? Has he had sex with a man? How does he manage the tremendous oppositions. I reached into my pocket to show him the kippah I had tucked away when I entered the center. It dawned on me suddenly that in the Gay and Lesbian Community Center I had become a closeted Orthodox Jew. Facing him in his Hasidic garb I grasped the irony of this "coming-out" encounter.

He agreed to speak with me for a few minutes. We went down the street to a diner for a cold drink, but he would not even drink the water. I asked him about his life. He said that he lived in two worlds. I asked if they ever touched each other. He said that recently he had trimmed his beard a quarter of an inch and let his bangs grow a bit as well. His ten-year-old daughter caught the meaning perfectly. Seeing him at some point in this hairstyle changed so slightly, she said, "Iz tati gevein a shegitz?" ("Is daddy becoming a Gentile?") I left Shmuel that afternoon amazed at the capacity of such a young man to live in two minds, two languages, two worlds so deftly.

Nine months later I was walking one warm Sunday afternoon in Soho and I stopped into the Center to munch on a muffin that I had just bought. There is a courtyard in back of the Center that is used by folks on sunny days as a place to bring a bagged lunch, to meet people, to hang out with a cup of coffee, or to read the paper. By this point in my coming-out process, I had decided that my kippah was not coming off. I made a blessing and began munching on my snack when I spotted a guy dressed in bicycle shorts, tank top, earrings, and a Caesar haircut. The rest of the crowd was dull in comparison to this guy, despite his gay-clone look, and for some reason, he seemed familiar to me. On my way out, I said hello, and he smiled back. I said, "Do I know you?" He answered, "Yes, Steve, its Shmuel."

"Shmuel?!" He explained that he had divorced his wife and had moved in with his Hispanic lover. He was learning a new trade having been blackballed from the diamond district. He dresses up just a bit to visit his kids. He does not keep kosher, nor is he Sabbath observant any longer. I asked him if he still believed that God gave the Torah at Sinai and that all Jews were duty-bound to fulfill it. He said, without hesitation, "Yes, but I simply cannot do it."

## Two Worlds

Shmuel preferred two independent pure worlds, even before he left his Jewish world for the gay world. Shmuel leaves the tradition unadulterated, if abandoned. In order to stay inside, I have had to tamper with the mold. For Shmuel, Jewish life is as sharply defined as gay life. Each has its customs of dress and rules of belonging. They are two pure and incommensurate worlds. My struggle became clearer to me at that moment with Shmuel. I understood that I was suited better to ambiguity rather than to pure belonging. Shmuel forced me to admit to myself that purity is part of the problem in the first place, that for me, the interpenetration of worlds is desirable.

However, if Shmuel was split in one way, I soon became split in another. If gay experience is part of God's creation, why, I began to ask, was it so reviled by God's law?

In the years of my painfully slow coming out, I was fitfully able to face myself as a gay man, but it was becoming much harder to face God. While I had begun to feel more at ease about myself, I began to feel terribly out of place in synagogue. The worst was Yom Kippur.

Every Yom Kippur gay Jews who attend services are faced with a dilemma. The dilemma is lost on those who show up for [only the prayer recitals] Kol Nidre in the evening and Neilah the following evening. Only those who essentially spend the whole day in synagogue confront this pain. In the afternoon service of Yom Kippur, the service of least attendance during the whole 24-hour-long marathon of prayer, the portion from Leviticus delineating the sexual prohibitions is read: "And with a male you shall not lie the lyings of a woman, it is an abomination."

I cringed to hear my shame read aloud on the Day of Atonement. The emotions accompanying the reading have changed through the years. At first, what I felt was guilt and contrition. Later, I felt a deep sadness for being caught up in gay desire and I would petition heaven for understanding. At other times, I would sob in my corner seat of the shul, acknowledging the pain of those verses upon my body and spirit. I have tried to connect myself with Jews of countless ages; listening in shul [the synagogue], their deepest feelings of love and desire turned abhorrent, ugly, and sinful. Finally, listening has become, in addition to all else I might feel, a protest.

During this entire period, I never missed the afternoon service on Yom Kippur. Never did I leave the synagogue for this gut-wrenching reading. It never dawned upon me to walk out. Over the years, I developed a sort of personal custom to stand up during the reading. I have always spent Yom Kippur in the seriously prayerful Orthodox environments. No one ever noticed me wrapped in my Kittel (a white cotton robe worn all day on Yom Kippur and in which pious Jews are buried when they die) with my tallit [prayer shawl] over my head, standing up for a single portion of a Torah reading, and crying.

## Journey Toward Integration

Finally on Yom Kippur 1996, I took my submission/protest one step further. I decided that it was not enough to stand up. I wanted to have the *aliyah* (to be called up to the Torah) for the reading of those very verses. I arranged with the *shamos* (a sexton) that I would have the proper *aliyah*, and when it was time, I went up [to] the bima [pedestal] in the center of the shul. My heart was pounding as I climbed the steps to the table, where the scroll is read. I felt as if I was standing on top of a mountain in a thunderstorm. My head was swirling as I looked out at the congregation seated around me. The men standing on each side of me at the podium were intent on their jobs, oblivious to me. Before me was the scroll.

It is hard to express the feeling of standing before an open Torah scroll. The Torah scroll possesses the highest level of sanctity of any object in a synagogue. If dropped, the whole congregation must fast. To stand there before the scroll as it is rolled open is both intensely intimate and public. I have studied this scroll for years. On [the] Simchat Torah [holiday], I have danced with it. I kiss it weekly as it passes through the congregation on Shabbat. The plaintive and magisterial melody of the reading on Yom Kippur is both ominous and comforting.

I said the blessing, the scroll is rolled open, and I am exposed. I hold on to the handles of the scroll for balance. I am surprised. The words are poetry. The uncovering of nakedness repeats as the language of sexual abuse. Thou shalt not uncover the nakedness of thy father's wife, or thy sister, or thy daughter-in-law, or aunt. I am aware of the power of this text on the Day of Atonement for all those who have been sexually abused. A day of healing cannot avoid enumerating the myriad ways that the intimacy of families can he turned into violence.

And then it comes. The horrible verse. To my surprise, when it is read, I no longer feel pain or even danger. I feel strangely empowered. By exposing myself to this verse, it has become exposed to me.

I finished the final blessing and the *shamos* [Rabbi's assistant], as is customary, begins to say the *mi sheberach*, a publicly spoken and somewhat self-styled blessing of healing that those who have *aliyot* [the honor of being called to read a blessing] are allowed to construct spontaneously: "He who blessed our ancestors . . . shall bless." And then one can fill in the blank and add whomever, one's own family members by name, the rabbi, the officers of the congregation, someone who needs assistance, anyone. The *shamos* begins the *mi sheberach* and waits for my cue. I say, "mishpachti (my family), the rabbi, officers of the synagogue, and their families . . . the whole congregation"—and pausing—*"v'kol holei AIDS b'tocheinu* and all those suffering from AIDS among us." The *shamos* froze. He rephrased my blessing, saying "and all those ill among us." I stopped him. No. This time I say it sharply and slowly: *"V'kol holei AIDS b'tocheinu."* He repeats my blessing word for word wanting to be finished with this already.

Standing amid the congregation, I felt the eyes of many upon me, but I was not looking at them. Gazing at the scroll, for the first time that I can remember, I felt it looking back at me.

In March of 1998, I came out of the closet in the Israeli paper *Maariv* as the first gay Orthodox rabbi. I formally came out to support a new gay and lesbian community center in the holy city, the Jerusalem Open House, which I had helped to found. While the timing was orchestrated by my desire to propel the Open House, I really came out because a switch had flipped in my mind. The closet, which had been the protector of my dignity, had become the armor of my shame. I was finally ready to defend the wholeness of my life, to stand up for the integrity and legitimacy of being who I am—a gay Orthodox rabbi.

# As a Gay African American, I Must Fight Internalized Homophobia

Geoffrey Giddings

Sharing their sexual orientation with heterosexual friends and family members can be a difficult process for many gays and lesbians. In the following essay Geoffrey Giddings explains how being African American made his "coming out" as a gay man even more of a challenge. The discovery of his sexual orientation made him realize that he had been taught to believe that African American and homosexual identities were incompatible. While studying both African and African American history in college, he developed pride in his racial heritage, but he hid his sexual orientation in shame. By confronting his own internalized homophobia, Giddings came to see how positive images of gay people are just as important to young homosexuals as positive African American images are to black youth.

My recent coming out to some friends and family members has caused me to think seriously about an important issue in my life and, I suspect, an issue that most homosexual men and women confront every day. Why is it so often painful to come out to straight people, even those who profess love for us? For me, dealing with this issue has taken a few years of fierce internal struggle before landing me at a place where my soul, mind, and conscience rest somewhat peacefully.

The first revelation of my sexuality to a straight person was my female best friend, Angela. I had been out of college one year and was about to begin teaching. Encouraged by a friend who was a tremendous source of inspiration, I felt that I should be more honest about my life to people I cared about. And, of course, close friends served as a good warm-up before I would let my family in on the big secret.

## Coming Out

I was petrified to reveal my deepest, darkest secret, even to one of my best friends. I was certain that Angela would be repulsed and would want to end our friendship. I actually looked forward to this reaction as an easy way out of the shame I imagined I would feel when discussing my sexuality with straight people. To my surprise she was open and understanding. She said she had suspected I was gay and that she had been afraid I would be offended if she asked. She was right; I would have been offended because I believed being thought of as gay meant I was being considered less than whole. I even felt ashamed that she had suspected me of being gay. I thought, Gee, what did I do to give myself away?

Angela's acceptance was no relief to me. Her acceptance meant that now I would have to deal with her knowing my secret. I thought this might mean she would always have thoughts of my being some sort of freak. Feelings of fear, guilt, and shame would always surface when hopeful but dejected female suitors asked if I were gay or when family members would pointedly inquire as to why I didn't have a girlfriend. So before coming out to other close friends and family members, I had to find some way of feeling more comfortable with my homosexuality.

After much thought, I began to realize that this confusion resulted from internalized heterosexism. Coming out to straight friends and family members was forcing me to reflect on a heated tension flaming within me, a tension ignited by the belief among many people of African descent that African and homosexual identities do not rightly coexist. It was only after my good friend nurtured my gay pride by introducing me to the works of Essex Hemphill and Joseph Beam that I worked up enough courage to reveal my sexuality to my two male college buddies after graduation. But the fact that I was not even in the same region of the country as they were helped me deal with the fear that they might lose respect for me, despite their outward acceptance.

## Growing Up

As a child my psyche had taken quite a beating. I received much teasing from my peers because of an early childhood skin disease. I held what I now view as a strange reverence for white cultural aesthetics and was attracted to only the lightest-skinned members of my community. The first attraction I had for a man was a light-skinned friend of my older brother. This preference for whiteness during early childhood years is fairly common among black children who are not taught to love themselves. In class I hear my students call their dark-skinned classmates "black" with utter disgust in their voices. . . .

I came to the States in 1980. My self-esteem was slowly strengthening as I began to excel academically. But strangely enough, this is the time I became aware that I was emotionally and sexually attracted to males. Throughout secondary school I secretly fantasized about males but did not have the confidence nor the encouragement to partake of the forbidden fruit. That didn't happen until well into my college career.

## Developing an Ethnic Identity

Five years at a predominantly white university forced me to seek self-affirmation from the few sisters and brothers on campus. It was in college that I learned just how intractable racism is in our society. In fact, my growing interest in my heritage inspired me to major in African and African-American history. The small nucleus of support made me comfortable. We all learned that knowledge is the key to overcoming the white cultural hegemony that made us unhappy on, and sometimes off, campus. Although I was well aware of my sexuality at this point, I believed nobody would understand, not even the openly gay folks, who were mostly white.

I refused to seek support from the white gay organization on campus. Despite the fact that this gay and lesbian organization was very popular and accepted by the entire campus community, I felt that whites could not help any African-American dealing with race issues, and certainly not a person of African descent who is struggling against the unique heterosexism found in the African/Caribbean-American communities.

So I locked myself up in the campus's microcosmic African-American community. It was there that I sought affirmation as a man of African descent to heal the scars I suffered when I was much younger. I realized I needed to build my self-esteem and what better way of doing that than by becoming proud of my African roots. This idea of acquiring positive self-esteem through knowledge of self and race pride is encouraged by such African-American social theorists as Dr. Jawanza Kunjufu and Dr. Molefi Kete Asante. By the end of my college years, I had come to see the benefits of this philosophy.

I became so in love with "blackness" that whenever I came down from school, family members teased me about always doing, reading, and talking about "black stuff." But when they finally realized my passion was not just a phase, the teasing stopped. I am proud that I have been able to encourage many people, including my older brothers, to seek out knowledge on the great legacy our forebears have left.

All this notwithstanding, I was becoming incredibly miserable. My self-esteem was not as strong as it should have been. I was too busy denying a very important part of myself.

Despite the fact that I was a socially well-adjusted person and still had no interest in dating girls, it was still assumed that I was straight simply because I was seen as a positive brother. I often took this assumption as a compliment because I had accepted the narrow definition of masculinity constructed by many in the African-American community. The result of this self-effacing compromise was that I encouraged heterosexism.

During my first year out of college, I attended a black men's support group sponsored by the Association of Black Psychologists, where the issue of homosexuality came up often. Each time it did, I simply shriveled up like a coward. I wanted to share my experience with those brothers because my story would have provided a unique perspective to them, most of whom did not believe they knew any gay person. But I feared that all the respect they had for me would have been thrown right out the door. Perhaps not, but I felt it was too risky. Thus, disassociation from my sexual reality was the price I paid to seek out and celebrate the riches of my heritage and to commune peacefully with my brothers and sisters.

## My Caribbean Heritage

In addition to my African ancestry, I am very proud of my Caribbean heritage. My chest swells when I think of my membership in a tradition that has produced the likes of Marcus Garvey, C.L.R. James, Walter Rodney, Kwame Toure, Michael Manley, Shirley Chisholm, and Derek Walcott. Living in Crown Heights in Brooklyn, New York, I was enveloped by Caribbean people: our styles, our languages, our beauty. However, what troubles me about this community is its pernicious heterosexism. This attitude of social intolerance and religion influencing fear and hate of homosexuality is well-documented. My family's attitude about homosexuality does not stray far from what is generally viewed as typical Caribbean heterosexism. When I think of coming out to my family I do not fear persecution. What I am truly afraid of is the incredible disappointment and shame family members would feel knowing there is an "antiman" in the family. As much as they love me, my family would detest being held accountable by neighbors and friends for having reared someone who violates their social and sexual tradition. What I also fear is the intense shame of homosexuality that even I myself have internalized after years of being told that it is something unclean and sinful.

Growing up in Guyana, I remember there was a flamboyant man whom we called Antiman Desmond, who would parade in fabulous costumes and dance in the Mashramani Independence Day carnivals. In retrospect, I find it strange but not surprising that as a child I never fathomed this man having a real life. I thought of him as just a jester, and that is what most people around me encouraged. I will admit, however, that part of me always admired this man, who seemed free to live as he wanted to. Nonetheless, the fact that Antiman Desmond was shunned by the community, sent a clear message to me that homosexuality is not a viable way to live. This is the sort of limited view of homosexuality that I felt I was up against whenever I considered coming out to my family.

As I continued to conceal my sexuality, a question that increasingly haunted me was how is it that a man with such strong race pride should suffer ambiguous feelings concerning his own sexuality. Asante and others had instilled a belief that when one is proud of one's heritage, one is almost emotionally unbeatable. But as I thought of how I viewed my sexuality, I realized that there was something lacking in this formula when applied to my feelings about myself as a homosexual man. I could stand tall and firmly announce my pride in being of African and Caribbean descent, but my head was cast down whenever I admired my homosexuality, even to myself. I began to be very critical of these insecure feelings of shame and fear. I started to see that my sexuality is very much an intrinsic part of who I am, and that the effects of heterosexism in our society can be personally as crippling as that of racism.

As Essex Hemphill said, "If I had read a book like *In the Life* [by Joseph Beam] when I was sixteen, there might have been one less mask for me to put aside later in life." Growing up, whether gay or straight, we are all naturally affirmed as heterosexuals by this society. Because of this fact, I believe that we older and more conscious homosexual men and women should take on the duty to do whatever is within our power to combat the damaging images of homosexuality this society perpetuates by affirming the natural sexuality of young people who are aware of their homosexuality. This is simply in sync with our long tradition of elders "looking after" the youth.

Accessibility to a network of gay role models among friends and associates is crucial to gay men and women in developing a positive self-identity. I have been fortunate to have developed a best friend and other good friends who are in the life. It is this sort of support I wish I had had earlier to affirm a self-image that is only now recovering from heterosexist abuse.

Now, some might wonder why come out at all. Why put oneself through the emotional fatigue and run the risk of being ostracized by friends and family. Well, the problem is, I want to send a clear message to all people I love that I would appreciate them loving me for the whole of who I am.

It is detrimental to my psychological well-being to be halted by feelings of shame and guilt whenever I think of simply being honest with my family about who I am. Sisters and brothers who fear the ramifications of coming out should be assured that there is support, strength, and salvation in numbers, unity, and consciousness. But ultimate responsibility for change lies with our larger community whose oppressive intolerance often forces us, especially our youth, to contemplate suicide. It is our duty as gay folks to help carry the torch to light America's path to becoming a truly just society. But before we take up the torch, many of us, myself included, need to be girded with the belief that our sexuality is a legitimate and beautiful reality, instead of something sinful and repulsive.

# A Lesbian Mother Talks to Her Son About Sexuality

Becky Thompson

Discussing the topic of sex with a child for the first time is not easy for many parents, but for Becky Thompson it was particularly complicated. Adrian, the fourth-grader she hoped to adopt, did not yet know she was gay. However, once he got past his initial surprise, Adrian asked more questions about his future mother's identity as a lesbian. When his school introduced a special unit about gay and lesbian history, Adrian learned how Thompson could be a valuable resource for his homework assignments. As they continued to talk, Adrian was able to make connections between the homophobia his mother experienced and the racism he experienced as an African American. The following selection is Thompson's account of their discussions. Thompson is an associate professor of sociology at Simmons College in Boston and the author of *Mothering Without a Compass: White Mother's Love, Black Son's Courage.*

Sex education began in this family in the fall, when Adrian [the boy she was trying to adopt] and I were eating breakfast with Hannah [Becky's partner] and her daughter, Diana, at a local diner in Brookline—the Busy Bee, known for its fast short-order cooks, home fries made with real potatoes, and caustic and fearless waitresses. Once Adrian came, Hannah and I often took the kids to breakfast on Saturday mornings, partly to avoid having to cook or clean up. Mostly, though, we went after having realized that over meals, especially at restaurants, Adrian tended to bring up the hard stuff, raise the real issues, and offer the dirt on his latest quandaries.

Diana and Adrian jostled about which toys to bring into the restaurant and who would sit on the outside and inside seat of the lime green, Naugahyde booth. After we ordered the food, which Adrian considers the essential business, he asked me if two men could kiss. I asked him if both of them were at least sixteen. He said "Yes," he thought so. "Are both of them consenting as well? Do they both want to kiss?" I asked.

"Yes," Adrian said with a humph, looking at me with one of those why-do-you-have-to-use-such-complicated-language looks. "Well, if they are consenting and old enough, then they can go for it," I said back to Adrian.

## First Reactions

Adrian looks at Diana, Diana looks at Adrian, then Diana says, "That is what my mom and Becky do. They kiss." Diana continues with total clarity, "You know, a girl doing it with another girl. That means they are gay." Adrian looks at Diana, then at me, then at Hannah. He then points at Hannah and says in an incredulous whisper, "You? You're a lesbian?" "Yes," Hannah says calmly, with the confidence born of twenty-plus years of being an out lesbian with various long-term relationships along the way. Adrian says, "What?!" rolls his eyes, starts to stick his finger down his throat, and pretends to gag. My heart stops beating, totally unprepared for such a visceral reaction, not knowing that, at his age, he might well have mimicked choking with the mention of any kind of adult sexuality. For him and most other fourth-grade boys, sexuality is "just disgusting."

I reach over to Adrian, touch him lightly on his arm, and say, "It's okay. We can talk about it." I touch him, probably to assure myself as much as or more than him. Diana points to her mother and says, "Yeah, she's a lesbian," and then points to me—waving her finger back and forth, between Hannah and me—until Adrian figures out that if Hannah is a lesbian, and I am her partner, then I must be a lesbian, too. Hannah and I look at each other, smiling, trying not to burst into laughter, outed at a local breakfast diner in Boston by an eight-year-old girl who has been surrounded, since she was adopted as a toddler, by lesbians who love her—her mother and her mother's many friends.

The kids go back to their toys as I sit, worrying silently about how Adrian will now use this information. Hating that is where my mind goes. Will he somehow know *not* to bring it up during one of his weekly phone conversations with his mother? It is too risky for me to find out if she is homophobic, at least until I have the guardianship papers that, at that point, were still pending. I look at Hannah with searching eyes. Though we are obviously not able to have this conversation now, I desperately need Hannah to see my fear, so I am not alone with homophobia potentially aimed at Adrian and me.

## Homework Help

During Gay Pride Week at Silver Street School, the teachers offered children a number of ways to learn about gay and lesbian life, including conversations about famous gay authors and artists, a discussion of lesbian and gay families, and a talk about the school's commitment to justice and equality. Between the morning at the Busy Bee restaurant and the scheduled assembly honoring the gay men and lesbians at Silver Street School, Adrian had come home with a vocabulary sheet requiring him and me to look up many words together—"lesbian," "homophobia," "discrimination," "sexuality," "equality," "protest," and "heterosexism"—and to use them in sentences. We did the assignment sprawled out with a big red dictionary that I have been using since I was in college.

He loved that I knew so much about the subject, that I could tell him definitions that went beyond the ones in the dictionary. Yes, as we discovered, the dictionary says a lesbian is "a native or resident of Lesbos, an island of Greece." "That is true, Adrian," I tell him. "But there are also lesbians in Nigeria, where your uncle Kayode is from, and South Africa, where I have traveled recently, and Mexico, where your housemate is from, and Brazil, where women—lesbian and straight—wear bikinis that are so brief that 'why bother?'

"Yes, you are right, Adrian. 'Heterosexism' is not in this dictionary. Let's look at when this dictionary was published," I say, while showing him how to find the date of publication on a left-hand page close to the front of the book. First in 1969. Last edition in 1981. "Well," I tell him, "it would make sense that 'heterosexism' would not be in the dictionary in 1969. That was the same year as Stonewall, which is considered the beginning of the gay liberation movement in the United States, when a multiracial group of gays and lesbians, many of them drag queens and butches, took to the streets in protest of police harassment in bars in New York City. Close to where you were born in fact, Adrian, almost twenty years before you were born." Ancient history in his mind.

"It makes sense," I explain, "that the earlier editions wouldn't include a definition of 'heterosexism' since the social movement was just beginning then. But why not in the 1980s?" I ask Adrian. "There is really no excuse," he explains. "That is an example of heterosexism." I beam at him as he uses the term "heterosexism" correctly and in context.

As we work our way through the list, Adrian asks many questions: "When did you know you were a lesbian?" "How could Hannah be a lesbian, too? She's too old." In his mind, Hannah's age—fifty-four—seems to put her out of range of being sexual. So, I let him know that for many people—including Hannah and me—getting older makes them more, not less, in touch with their sexuality, desire, and whom they love.

## Lesbian Status Symbol

By the time the assembly honoring gay and lesbian awareness day came to Silver Street, I had clearly come to be a status symbol—albeit a temporary one—in Adrian's mind. As an out lesbian at the school, I was someone Adrian could claim that week. Because of me, he had

special knowledge—the insider's scoop. Because of me, he would definitely have a special reason to be at the assembly. Because of our conversation, he had, so the teachers told me later, the confidence to talk
more in class that week than he had so far during the fall.

I marvel at how it is that Adrian came to understand my sexuality
first through a gay- and lesbian-friendly curriculum at his school. And
how that timing was so unique to our particular situation. Had he been
living with me longer, his knowledge about lesbians might have first
been through his being teased by his peers. Chances are his first interac-
tions might have begun on the defensive—having to protect himself
and me from teasing or to separate from me in some painful way.

Before he came to Silver Street, I think he knew very little. I had
said almost nothing to him, believing that he would ask when he was
ready. I was hesitant about being explicit for fear that he might talk
about it with his mother or grandmother before I was ready. My heart
was very full the day of the assembly as parents filed in to watch the
event. An eclectic and colorful group of parents had made it their
business to come—straight, lesbian, gay, and bisexual. And the children clearly seemed joyful about this day of celebration.

## Making Connections

Most important of all for me, though, was how the week on gay and
lesbian lives helped Adrian find a way to talk with me about race and
racism for the first time. It was when he asked me about examples of
heterosexism that he first offered his own feelings about racism. It
was when I said that not everyone can be counted on to deal well
with issues of prejudice against gays and lesbians that he talked about
not trusting very many people to understand the isolation and hurt
he feels as an African American child. In my college classes, I teach
about the power of bridge work—how knowing about one oppression
can, in some situations, lead people to want to learn about other
oppressions. But to see Adrian reach toward his knowledge of racism
to let me know that he understood heterosexism, to see that his outrage when I told him about gay-bashing could help him see why I
would feel outrage about racist violence, convinced me like never
before of the power of bridge work as a translator of experience.

# I Was Gay

Stephen Bennett

In this selection, Stephen Bennett describes how his first homosexual encounter plunged him into depression, alcohol and drug abuse, bulimia, and homosexual promiscuity. Seven years later he hit bottom and entered a drug rehabilitation program. He eventually became alcohol, drug-free, and bulimia free but continued to live as a gay man. It was not until a close friend advised him to accept Jesus Christ as his savior that he began to seriously question the morality of his sexual preference. When he decided to live as a Christian, he was able to repair his relationship with his estranged father, marry a Christian woman, and build a family that includes two children. In 2000 Bennett founded Stephen Bennett Ministries, Inc. in Huntington, Connecticut, an organization that promotes traditional family values and runs a biblical recovery program for those who want to overcome their unwanted same-sex attractions.

In the fall of 1981, as an 18 year old aspiring artist with a dream, and a freshman at one of New York's art schools, I reached one of the darkest periods in my life. On a cold rainy night, far away from home I acted out on feelings I had throughout my entire childhood and teen years—I had my first homosexual encounter with another student. After drinking alcohol at a school party and getting drunk for the first time ever, something I swore I never would do because of my family's past, my life literally changed in one night. I was plummeted into the deep dark world of homosexuality.

After only a few short months in art school, I suffered from a very severe depression and dropped out of school and returned home to my family in Connecticut.

I found many of my old high school friends had also "come out" as homosexuals, and became very active in the homosexual bar scene. I lived for the night—my drinking became worse, I started using cocaine to help alleviate my mental turmoil, and found much love and acceptance by other men. I had many numerous one night stands. I felt I

Stephen Bennett, "God's Amazing Grace: The Testimony of Stephen Bennett," www. SBMinistries.org, 2002. Copyright © 2002 by Stephen Bennett Ministries. Reproduced by permission.

was finally "me." However, my drug addiction got worse to the point where I became a cocaine dealer just to support my habit—I lost my art business to drugs, as well as my dignity to a life based upon a perverse, sensual and decrepit lifestyle I couldn't break free from. It was at this point many of my friends and one night encounters were getting sick and dying, and no one knew why. This sickness was the beginning of the AIDS epidemic.

## On the Road to Recovery

Things only grew worse and for a period of 6 years I declined morally, mentally and physically. It was in the winter of 1987 after a 3 day cocaine and alcohol binge I cried out for help. After being up all night and running out of cocaine, I looked in the mirror and was shocked at the reflection. Due to my cocaine abuse, as well as years of bulimia, at almost 6 feet tall, I saw a 135 lb. living skeleton staring back at me, and I began to cry. I ran down to a payphone on the corner and called for help. I admitted myself into a drug rehabilitation program, and began my recovery as an inpatient for 3 months at a nearby facility. It was at this point I began to see God working in my life.

Within a few short months I was alcohol and drug free, as well as freed from my bulimia. I had gained about 25 lbs. and was feeling great. However, I still had a deep dark secret past hidden inside of me. What was I to do with my homosexuality? Deep down inside I knew it was wrong, yet I was just suppressing it. After dating a few girls, I found myself one night back again at a local gay bar. I didn't drink—but that night I met a man that I fell in love with, and began a 3 year live in relationship with him.

It seemed I had it all—my homosexual lifestyle and love, without the drugs, alcohol and bulimia, a great job, beautiful home, and great homosexual friends. I attended church faithfully every week—and felt I had it all. But God wasn't done with me yet—in fact, He had just started.

My doorbell rang, and it was my friend Kathy, a friend for years who had seen me through the good and bad times of my life—and she had a Bible in her hand, and asked if she could come in. She had told me she left her religious background and became a Christian. She told me how Jesus changed her life, and how according to the Bible homosexuality was wrong—it was a sin and an abomination in God's eyes—how according to the Bible I was not "born that way"—and that Jesus could set me free—today. I listened intently, and something inside of me told me she was right. I told her I would take the Bible and she left.

That day, the Word of God cut right through me—I saw my homosexuality for the first time as God saw it—*as sin*. Anytime something would happen between me and my partner sexually, I found myself praying for forgiveness to God on my bathroom floor. God was tugging at my heart strings, and I knew it.

The tugging was so hard and clear, I left my partner, my job, my family—everything—and headed off to Provincetown, MA—a homosexual subculture—to live for a summer, to see if I could reconcile this pull between being a homosexual and a Christian. Did I have to choose one or the other, or could I be both at the same time in God's eyes?

Well, in that summer of 1991 God opened my eyes to the truth and perverseness of the homosexual lifestyle. I saw it all in full swing, in all its glory—transsexuals, transvestites, sadomasochists—men and women doing things one would never even imagine.

After 5 months in Provincetown, I returned home to my partner asking for forgiveness for leaving him—I was sorry and I was going to put this "Christian" business aside. After only 4 short months at home in his house, by myself while wrapping Christmas presents, I happened to flip through radio stations and came across a Christian one. A man was singing a song and I heard the lyrics about "men marching for their right to sin." I knew exactly what the song was talking about—*it was talking about me.* I may have put God on the back burner—but He was still chasing after me.

## A Cry for Help

On New Year's eve I attended a homosexual party with my partner, and for the first time ever in my life—I felt "dirty." I hated myself. I hated my lifestyle. But I just couldn't break free. . . .

I called my friend Kathy on the telephone, and told her I was going to move back to Provincetown, MA for good and completely give myself over to the homosexual lifestyle. I felt as if I lost my soul—I was crying out for help—and that's when Jesus Christ stepped in.

She read to me from the Bible, from the book of Romans, how God will "call" you—and if He keeps calling you, and you hear, yet harden your heart, it may come to a point where He will make you a "reprobate" in His sight and give you completely over to your sin, and allow you to believe "the lie." At that point, according to the Bible, you have basically sealed your destiny away from Him forever.

It scared me so much, I asked her what I needed to do, and she told me right now to pray to Jesus—ask Him to deliver me from the homosexuality—and Him to forgive me for my sins, and to come into my heart and life, be my Lord and Savior, and to take control. At that moment, I did and physically felt the peace of God upon me. That day in January of 1992, on the telephone, I asked Jesus to come into my heart—and He set me free. That day God changed my life forever and I will be eternally grateful to Him for what He did. Within 2 weeks of that time I moved out of my partner's home and was on my way and walk with Jesus Christ.

Within 2 months of accepting Jesus Christ as my Savior, I knew deep down I had to deal with the root cause of my homosexuality in order to move on with my life. For me, it was a broken relationship with my father.

## Building New Relationships

For years, I only desired one thing: my father's love. I knew as Jesus had forgiven me for all of my sins—past, present and future—I now needed to extend that forgiveness that I received—to my father. After confronting him one day, pouring out my heart and really talking for the very first time—our broken relationship was reconciled. Forgiveness was extended and the chains that bound me for years were unshackled.

Today, my father and I have a wonderful relationship. I love my dad and I know he loves me. I realized for all of those years, I was vainly looking for the love of my father in the arms of other men. Today, the search is over: *I have the real thing.*

I must say, it is incredible how my journey has been. Within that first year, I was engaged to a beautiful Christian woman, Irene, who knew me as a homosexual, and was praying for me for years. We were married on June 13, 1993. Today, over eleven years later—and very happily married—God has blessed us with two other miracles—my beautiful daughter Chloe Catherine who is 7 years old, and my son Blake Stephen, 5 years old, born on Chloe's birthday. Chloe's middle name is in dedication to my friend Kathy who never gave up on me— a vessel of God, who He used to change my destiny forever.

Today life is wonderful—I am free, and it is all because of Jesus Christ and His love for me. Jesus is the answer for all of our needs, no matter what they are. You may be, know or live with a homosexual, a drug addict, or an alcoholic. Understand—God loves the sinner—He just hates the sin.

Remember, with God, nothing is impossible—believe me, I know. I do believe in miracles—I believe in miracles, for I've seen a soul set free . . . for that lost soul was *me.*

# Unapologetically Christian, Unapologetically Lesbian

Anita Cadonau-Huseby

Some believe that Christians cannot be homosexual. In her traditional upbringing, Anita Cadonau-Huseby was taught that being both Christian and a lesbian was an impossible contradiction. As a full-time minister in a conservative church, she experienced great inner turmoil and fear for her career when she realized she was attracted to other women. She has since come to believe that being a lesbian does not preclude her from also being an evangelical Christian. Cadonau-Huseby currently lives with her life partner and serves as an ordained minister in the Disciples of Christ Church.

Unapologetically Christian. Unapologetically Lesbian. *It's not a contradiction. Neither are you.*

I like that. If I had the money I'd put it up on billboards across America and if I ever win the lottery maybe I'll do just that. I suppose I need to actually play the lottery to raise my odds on winning but that's neither here nor there.

When I wrote that short little phrase, and as I write this essay I'm thinking of you who fervently believe there's no such thing as a "Christian lesbian." You consider the term to be an oxymoron but more than that, you regard it an offense to the Gospel. You believe if someone really is a Christian they will seek repentance from the sin of homosexuality and will do all they can to change and short of change they will at least commit to a life of celibacy.

I also have those of you in mind who, even while doubting such a thing as a "Christian lesbian" can exist you've admitted to yourself that while you love Jesus and are committed to the Christian life, your only desire in an intimate and loving relationship is with another woman. Because of this apparent conflict you feel as though there's a choice you're going to eventually be forced to make, either to walk away from your faith in God or to deny, reject, or attempt to change your attraction to other women. If that's the personal struggle you're secretly holding in your heart then I'm writing to you.

And to both of you I'm writing as someone who knows you well because at one time I was you. For most of my life I believed homosexuality to be a grievous sin that led good people astray from a true faith in God. When a friend confessed her feelings toward another woman I prayed faithfully for her, counseled her, and rejoiced when her homosexual relationship ended. It was out of love and compassion and my strong belief in what I saw the Bible to clearly say about homosexuality that I reached out to help a friend I feared was slipping away from God and toward a life of destruction. A few years later, I found myself engaged in an internal conflict I have never before known and that I could never have imagined. Above all else I was a committed Christian whose greatest longing was to live in a manner that brought honor to God but suddenly I recognized my lifelong unnamed feelings as being the very thing that would bring the most disappointment to the heart of God. I told no one so great was my shame and spent my evening hours crying out to God in prayers full of promise. I will change. I will do whatever it takes. I will never do anything to disgrace you. I will die before I do. And prayers of pleading. Please forgive me for whatever I did to make this happen. Change me. Help me. Don't leave me. Please don't hate me. In that moment I looked down the path of my future and saw nothing good.

I really have been there. I really have said and done and felt that. So to you, whoever you are, I want to offer a very basic response to this whole debate around being Christian and being gay. Let's call this little explanatory essay of mine "Christian Lesbian 101: The Basics."

## I Am a Christian

I'm not attempting here to explain Christianity to those outside the Christian faith. I consider myself to be an evangelical Christian in the sense that I love, and am committed to, sharing my faith with others. I really do consider it the Good News and I've never been one to keep from sharing anything for which I have passion. For the purpose of this essay and for the sake of brevity I'm going to use religious-sounding language that I normally would avoid or need to explain in a conversation with someone of another faith just as I would need them to explain their own set of religious terminology that was centered in their own faith tradition. Here I'm directing my words to those of you who already identify as Christians.

When I say I'm a Christian I'm recognizing both a past event and a present reality. There was one moment in the past when I made the conscious and deliberate choice to acknowledge Jesus as my Savior and Lord. As my Savior, Jesus through his life, death and resurrection forgave my sins, restored my relationship with God and secured for me the promise of everlasting life. With Jesus as my Lord I submit my will daily to His will, seeking God's plan for my life rather than my own. I'm a Christian, not by my own virtue but by the completed work of Christ (See John 11:25, John 5:24, Acts 2:38, John 20:31, Romans 1:16, Ephesians 2:8,9 and Colossians 1:21–23). In all these passages scripture seems relatively clear that while the final choice was mine everything else was left up to Jesus and if that's the case my salvation doesn't hinge on my faith or adherence in church teaching or in those dogmas and doctrines that are nonessential to the finished work of Calvary. It is about Christ and Christ crucified alone and to add conditions or requirements onto that glorious reality is to imply that the death and resurrection of Jesus was insufficient. While a church might say "Believe as we believe and do as we do and you can join us here" Jesus welcomes all who love Him and humbly seek Him.

## I Am a Lesbian

While I remember the very place and time when at the age of five I became a Christian, there was never a single moment when I made a conscious choice to be a lesbian and I always take it with a mix of mild amusement and irritation when people will argue that it was a choice. My irritation is that people who don't live inside my own skin would be so arrogant as to presume they know what happened within me better than I do and the amusement is in those moments when I play with the thought of how fun it would be to call them some morning asking "So how am I feeling today?" They should know after all.

And let's talk about this choice. At the time I realized I was a lesbian I was firmly grounded within conservative Christianity, both in my family and within the church where I served in full-time ministry. I had a large circle of friends, a lovely home, and a wonderful future in ministry that I loved and that brought my parents great pride and joy. Had you posed my life as a hypothetical situation and asked me what I thought would happen to someone who came out in that setting as a homosexual I would have been able to describe in detail the graphic consequences. I had a history in the church and so I'd seen the church and its people respond to those considered "in sin" and it was never pretty or kind and it was definitely nothing I ever wanted to experience firsthand. Now, I'm not the brightest bulb on the tree but I have enough intelligence to avoid certain choices like sticking my wet thumb into a light switch, coating my body with honey and lying on an ant hill or doing or being anything that's going to upset and repulse everyone I love and cause my dismissal from the only community I have ever known. Most of the gay and lesbian people I know seem to possess the same level of logic and self-preservation.

I'm in a committed relationship with my life partner Dana. We've been together for two years and will be getting married in a Christian wedding at a church. Our marriage will be affirmed by God and the church where our union will be celebrated even though the state will fail to recognize it. There's nothing about our life together that would look strange or odd were Dana a man and our relationship heterosexual. As a Christian couple, we begin each morning by reading devotions together. I cook breakfast. Dana makes the bed. We shower, dress and go to work. During the day we call each other to express our love or to remind the other to pick up more milk on the way home. After the dinner dishes are put away, we watch television or play with the kitten or just putter around the house until bedtime when we fall asleep beside the other. There's nothing bizarre about our life. Nothing unusual. While some would even consider our lives boring I treasure each day as an amazing and joyful blessing.

And yet, there is something very different about being a lesbian in this world. Being lesbian means knowing that in certain parts of this country you can't hold your partner's hand in public like straight couples do without risking being ridiculed or assaulted. Being lesbian means picking up the paper every morning or watching the news every night to hear about some new legislation that's being debated that if passed would negatively impact your life. Being lesbian means listening to false stereotypes being painted about you and the people you love every Sunday morning by television evangelists, all in the name of God. Being lesbian means trying to explain the nonexistence of the homosexual lifestyle or agenda to strangers.

But being lesbian means even more. Being lesbian means celebrating the joy of being a woman. Being lesbian means giving full expression to the depths of the love within you. Being lesbian means living confidently with God's approval rather than with the approval of others. Being a lesbian means standing in solidarity with others who stand on the outside whether they be the poor, the sick, the elderly, or any among God's creation deemed not acceptable by the majority. Being lesbian means finding your courage and living boldly. Being lesbian means experiencing another woman's courage when she takes your hand in a roomful of strangers or shows her engagement ring proudly without embarrassment or thought to what others will think.

I am a Christian. That is my faith. I am a lesbian. That is my sexual orientation. I make no apology for being either and if after all is said and done I remain a contradiction to you then that's fine too. Just realize what that means. When I speak of the presence of Jesus in my life you need to reject it. You have to see the fruit of the Holy Spirit within my life and call it evil. You have to deny the sufficiency of salvation through faith by requiring that I be heterosexual to first receive it. Maybe you're right and I'm just not getting it and I never will. Perhaps I'm just foolish and naive enough to believe I can have it all, that I can live in wholeness and in relationship with God. So far that's what I've experienced and it's been the most joyful and God-filled adventure of my life!

# ORGANIZATIONS TO CONTACT

The editors have compiled the following list of organizations concerned with the issues debated in this book. The descriptions are derived from materials provided by the organizations. All have publications or information available for interested readers. The list was compiled on the date of publication of the present volume; names, addresses, phone and fax numbers, and e-mail and Internet addresses may change. Be aware that many organizations take several weeks or longer to respond to inquiries, so allow as much time as possible.

### Alliance Defense Fund (ADF)
15333 North Pima Rd., Suite 165, Scottsdale, AZ 85260
(800) 835-5233 • fax: (480) 444-0025
Web site: www.alliancedefensefund.org

ADF provides funding, legal support, and training to organizations that support conservative Christian values, religious freedom, and the traditional family in the United States. It trains church and civic leaders to fight against same-sex marriage, legalized abortion, and assisted suicide. ADF conducts the National Litigation Academy to educate attorneys and provide pro bono legal assistance in national and local cases.

### American Civil Liberties Union (ACLU) Lesbian and Gay Rights Project
125 Broad St., New York, NY 10004
(212) 549-2627
Web site: www.aclu.org/LesbianGayRights/LesbianGayRightsmain.cfm

The ACLU is the nation's oldest and largest civil liberties organization. Its Lesbian and Gay Rights Project, started in 1986, handles litigation, education, and public policy work on behalf of gays and lesbians. The union supports same-sex marriage. It publishes the monthly newsletter *Civil Liberties Alert*, the handbook *The Rights of Lesbians and Gay Men*, the briefing paper *Lesbian and Gay Rights*, and the books *The Rights of Families: The ACLU Guide to the Rights of Today's Family Members* and *Making Schools Safe: An Anti-Harassment Training Program for Schools*.

### Canadian Lesbian and Gay Archives
Box 639, Station A, Toronto, ON M5W 1G2 Canada
(416) 777-2755
Web site: www.clga.ca

The archives collects and maintains information and materials relating to the gay and lesbian rights movement in Canada and elsewhere. Its collection of records and other materials documenting the stories of lesbians and gay men and their organizations in Canada is available to the public for the purpose of education and research. It has published numerous books and pamphlets and publishes an annual newsletter, *Lesbian and Gay Archivist*.

### Children of Lesbians and Gays Everywhere (COLAGE)
3543 Eighteenth St. #1, San Francisco, CA 94110
(415) 861-KIDS (5437) • fax: (415) 255-8345
Web site: www.colage.org/index.html

COLAGE is an international organization to support young people with gay, lesbian, bisexual, or transgendered parents. It coordinates pen pal and scholarship programs and sponsors an annual Family Week to celebrate family diversity. COLAGE publishes a quarterly newsletter and maintains several e-mail discussion lists.

### Concerned Women for America (CWA)
1015 Fifteenth St. NW, Suite 1100, Washington, DC 20005
(202) 488-7000 • fax: (202) 488-0806
Web site: www.cwfa.org

The CWA is an educational and legal defense foundation that seeks to strengthen the traditional family by applying Judeo-Christian moral standards. It opposes gay marriage and the granting of additional civil rights protections to gays and lesbians. It publishes the monthly magazine *Family Voice* and various position papers on gay marriage and other issues.

### Equal Marriage for Same-Sex Couples
Kevin Bourassa and Joe Varnell in care of:
Bruce E. Walker Law Office
65 Wellesley St. E, Suite 205, Toronto, ON M4Y 1G7 Canada
(416) 961-7451
Web site: www.samesexmarriage.ca

Equal Marriage was started in 2001 by Kevin Bourassa and Joe Varnell when their Toronto Metropolitan Community Church went to court in Ontario, Canada, seeking government recognition of civil gay marriage. The organization, a clearinghouse for legal information about same-sex marriage in Canada and the United States, is a center for legal and social action and publishes an e-mail newsletter.

### Families Like Mine
1730 New Brighton Blvd., PMB 175, Minneapolis, MN 55413
(866) 245-4281
Web site: http://familieslikemine.com

Families Like Mine is a Web site dedicated to decreasing isolation for people who have parents who are lesbian, gay, bisexual, or transgender. Created by Abigail Gardner, author of *Families Like Mine: Children of Gay Parents Tell It Like It Is,* the site offers testimonies, resources, and the monthly newsletter *E-News.*

### Family Pride Coalition
PO Box 65327, Washington, DC 20035
(202) 331-5015 • fax: (202) 331-0080
Web site: www.familypride.org

The Family Pride Coalition advocates for the well-being of lesbian, gay, bisexual, and transgendered (LGBT) parents and their families through mutual support, community collaboration, and public understanding. It lobbies for positive public policy, educates communities about LGBT families, and provides information for LGBT families to enhance their lives. Family Pride publishes numerous pamphlets, such as *How to Talk to Children About Our Families,* and the quarterly newsletter *Family Tree.*

### Family Research Council (FRC)
801 G St. NW, Washington, DC 20001
(202) 393-2100 • fax: (202) 393-2134
Web site: www.frc.org

The Family Research Council is a research and educational organization that promotes the traditional family, which the council defines as a group of people bound by marriage, blood, or adoption. The council opposes gay marriage and adoption rights. It publishes numerous reports from a conservative perspective on issues affecting the family, including *Free to Be Family*. Among its other publications are the monthly newsletters *State of the Family* and *Washington Watch* and the semiannual journal *Family Policy Review*.

### Family Research Institute (FRI)
PO Box 62640, Colorado Springs, CO 80962
(303) 681-3113
Web site: www.familyresearchinst.org

The FRI distributes information about family, sexual, and substance abuse issues. The institute believes that strengthening traditional marriage would reduce many social problems, including crime, poverty, and sexually transmitted diseases. The FRI publishes the monthly newsletter *Family Research Report* as well as the pamphlets *Same-Sex Marriage: Til Death Do Us Part??* and *Homosexual Parents: A Comparative Study*.

### Focus on the Family
8685 Explorer Dr., Colorado Springs, CO 80920
(719) 531-3400 • (800) 232-6459
Web site: www.family.org

Focus on the Family is a Christian organization that seeks to strengthen the traditional family in America and opposes gay marriage. It believes that the family is the most important social unit and maintains that reestablishing the traditional two-parent family will end many social problems. In addition to conducting research and educational programs, Focus on the Family publishes the monthly periodicals *Focus on the Family* and *Citizen* as well as the reports *Setting the Record Straight: What Research Really Says About the Consequences of Homosexuality* and *Twice as Strong: The Undeniable Advantages of Raising Children in a Traditional Two-Parent Family*.

### Gay & Lesbian Alliance Against Defamation (GLAAD)
248 W. Thirty-fifth St., 8th Fl., New York, NY 10001
(212) 629-3322 • fax: (212) 629-3225
Web site: www.glaad.org

GLAAD works to promote fair, accurate, and inclusive representation in the media as a means of eliminating homophobia and discrimination based on gender identity and sexual orientation. The organization publishes the online newsletters *GLAAD Alert* and *Calls to Action*, a *Media Reference Guide*, and training manuals to educate people about responsible and evenhanded media.

### Gay, Lesbian and Straight Education Network (GLSEN)
121 W. Twenty-seventh St., Suite 804, New York, NY 10001
(212) 727-0135 • fax: (212) 727-0254
Web site: www.glsen.org

GLSEN is a national nonprofit organization that develops and implements policies to ensure safe schools for gay, lesbian, bisexual, and transgendered students and teachers. GLSEN conducts an annual conference and distributes Respect Awards to honor leaders who promote acceptance of all people in educational settings. The organization publishes articles such as "Is This the Right School for Us?" and curriculum guides, including *At Issue: Exploring the Debate over Marriage Rights for Same-Sex Couples* and *How Does Homophobia Hurt Us All?*

## Human Rights Campaign (HRC)
1640 Rhode Island Ave. NW, Washington, DC 20036
(202) 628-4160
Web site: www.hrc.org/Template.cfm?Section=About_HRC_FamilyNet

HRC is a clearinghouse for information for lesbian, gay, bisexual, and trans-gendered families coordinated by the Human Rights Campaign Foundation. It provides information and resources about adoption, civil unions, coming out, custody and visitation, donor insemination, family law, families of origin, gay marriage, money, parenting, religion, schools, senior health and housing, state laws and legislation, straight spouses, and transgender and workplace issues. HRC publishes numerous reports and the *HRC FamilyNet News*.

## Lambda Legal Defense and Education Fund
120 Wall St., Suite 1500, New York, NY 10005
(212) 809-8585 • fax: (212) 809-0055
Web site: www.lambdalegal.org

Lambda is a public interest law firm committed to achieving full recognition of the civil rights of lesbians, gay men, and people with HIV/AIDS. The firm addresses a variety of topics, including equal marriage rights, parenting and relationship issues, and domestic partner benefits. It believes that marriage is a basic right and an individual choice. Lambda publishes the quarterly *Lambda Update*, the pamphlet *Feedom to Marry*, and position papers on same-sex marriage and gay and lesbian family rights.

## National Association for Research and Therapy of Homosexuality (NARTH)
16633 Ventura Blvd., Suite 1340, Encino, CA 91436-1801
(818) 789-4440 • fax: (818) 789-6452
Web site: www.narth.com

Founded in 1992 by former psychiatrist Charles W. Socarides, NARTH is a non-profit organization dedicated to affirming a traditional heterosexual model of gender and sexuality. NARTH provides educational resources and a therapist referral to homosexuals who seek to become heterosexual. It publishes a news-letter called *NARTH Bulletin* three times a year and distributes pamphlets and position papers such as *Sexual Politics and Scientific Logic: The Issues of Homosexuality* and *Homosexual Advocacy Groups & Your School*.

## National Center for Lesbian Rights (NCLR)
870 Market St., Suite 570, San Francisco, CA 94102
(415) 392-8442
Web site: www.nclrights.org

The National Center for Lesbian Rights is a public interest law office that provides legal counseling and representation to victims of sexual orientation discrimination. Primary areas of advice include child custody and parenting, employment, housing, the military, and insurance. Among the center's publications are the pamphlets *Same-Sex Relationship Recognition* and *Adoption by Lesbian, Gay, Bisexual, and Transgender Parents: An Overview of the Current Law*.

## National Gay and Lesbian Task Force (NGLTF)
1325 Massachusetts Ave. NW, Suite 600, Washington, DC 20005
(202) 393-5177 • fax: (202) 393-2241
Web site: www.ngltf.org

The NGLTF is a civil rights advocacy organization that lobbies Congress and the White House on a range of civil rights and AIDS issues affecting gays and lesbians. The organization is working to make same-sex marriage legal. It publishes numerous papers and pamphlets, the booklets *Family Policy: Issues Affecting Gay, Lesbian, Bisexual and Transgender Families* and *Massachusetts Equal Marriage Rights Policy Brief,* and the quarterly *Task Force Report.*

### Parents, Friends, and Families of Lesbians and Gays (P-FLAG)
1726 M St. NW, Suite 400, Washington, DC 20036
(202) 467-8180 • fax: (202) 467-8194
Web site: www.pflag.org

P-FLAG is a national organization that provides support and education services for gays, lesbians, bisexuals, transgendered people, and their families and friends. It also works to end prejudice and discrimination against homosexuals. It publishes and distributes pamphlets and articles, including *Faith in Our Families, Our Daughters and Sons: Questions and Answers for Parents of Gay, Lesbian, Bisexual, and Transgendered People,* and *Hate Crimes Hurt Families.*

### Religious Coalition for the Freedom to Marry (RCFM)
325 Huntington Ave., Suite 88, Boston, MA 02115-4401
(617) 848-9900
Web site: www.RCFM.org

The Religious Coalition for the Freedom to Marry supports civil marriage rights for same-gender couples and seeks to promote dialogue within faith communities about religious marriage for gay and lesbian couples. Its members include Baptists, Mormons, Jews, Lutherans, Presbyterians, Quakers, Buddhists, and Episcopalians. RCFM educates communities, lobbies legislatures, and circulates for signatures the "Massachusetts Declaration of Religious Support for the Freedom of Same-Sex Couples to Marry."

### Traditional Values Coalition (TVC)
139 C St. SE, Washington, DC 20003
(202) 547-8570 • fax: (202) 546-6403
Web site: www.traditionalvalues.org

The Traditional Values Coalition strives to restore what the group believes are the traditional moral and spiritual values in American government, schools, media, and society. It believes that gay marriage threatens the family unit and extends civil rights beyond what the coalition considers appropriate limits. The coalition publishes the newsletter *TVC Weekly News* as well as various information papers addressing same-sex marriage and other issues.

# BIBLIOGRAPHY

## Books

Jean M. Baker — *How Homophobia Hurts Children: Nurturing Diversity at Home, at School, and in the Community.* New York: Harrington Park, 2002.

Jack O. Balswick, Judith K. Balswick, and Judy Balswick — *The Family: A Christian Perspective on the Contemporary Home.* Grand Rapids, MI: Baker Book House, 1999.

Paul Beeman — *In Your Face: Stories from the Lives of Queer Youth.* New York: Columbia University Press, 2000.

Nijole V. Benokraitus — *Feuds About Families: Conservative, Centrist, Liberal, and Feminist Perspectives.* New York: Prentice-Hall, 1999.

Robert A. Bernstein, Betty DeGeneres, and Robert MacNeil — *Straight Parents, Gay Children: Keeping Families Together.* New York: Thunder's Mouth, 2003.

Stephanie A. Brill — *The Queer Parent's Primer: A Lesbian and Gay Families' Guide to Navigating Through a Straight World.* Oakland, CA: New Harbinger, 2001.

Christopher Carrington — *No Place Like Home: Relationships and Family Life Among Lesbians and Gay Men.* Chicago: University of Chicago Press, 1999.

Hayden Curry, Frederick Hertz, and Denis Clifford — *A Legal Guide for Lesbian and Gay Couples.* Berkeley, CA: NOLO, 2004.

William N. Eskridge Jr. — *Equality Practice: Civil Unions and the Future of Gay Rights.* New York: Routledge, 2001.

Byrne Fone — *Homophobia: A History.* New York: Metropolitan, 2000.

Abigail Garner — *Families Like Mine: Children of Gay Parents Tell It Like It Is.* New York: HarperCollins, 2004.

Evan Gerstmann — *Same-Sex Marriage and the Constitution.* New York: Cambridge University Press, 2003.

Richard Goldstein — *The Attack Queers: Liberal Society and the Gay Right.* New York: Verso, 2002.

Lynn Haley-Banez and Joanne Garrett — *Lesbians in Committed Relationships: Extraordinary Couples, Ordinary Lives.* New York: Harrington Park, 2002.

Daniel A. Helminiak — *What the Bible Really Says About Homosexuality.* San Francisco: Alamo Square, 2000.

Anne Hendershott and Jorge Masetti — *The Politics of Deviance.* San Francisco: Encounter Books, 2004.

| | |
|---|---|
| Noelle Howey and Ellen Samuels, eds. | *Out of the Ordinary: Essays on Growing Up with Gay, Lesbian, and Transgender Parents*. New York: St. Martin's, 2000. |
| Janet R. Jakobsen and Ann Pellegrini | *Love the Sin: Sexual Regulation and the Limits of Tolerance*. Boston: Beacon, 2004. |
| Moises Kaufman | *The Laramie Project*. New York: Vintage Books, 2001. |
| Kevin K. Kumashiro | *Troubling Education: "Queer" Activism and Anti-Oppressive Pedagogy*. London: Falmer Press, 2002. |
| Robert Lewis and Stu Weber | *Raising a Modern Day Knight: A Father's Role in Guiding His Son to Authentic Manhood*. Colorado Springs, CO: Focus on the Family, 1999. |
| Arthur Lipkin | *Understanding Homosexuality, Changing Schools*. Boulder, CO: Westview, 2000. |
| Gerald P. Mallon | *Gay Men Choosing Parenthood*. New York: Columbia University Press, 2004. |
| Eric Marcus | *What If Someone I Know Is Gay? Answers to Questions About Gay and Lesbian People*. New York: Price Stern Sloan, 2000. |
| Michael Mello | *Legalizing Gay Marriage: Vermont and the National Debate*. Philadelphia: Temple University Press, 2004. |
| David Moats | *Civil Wars: Gay Marriage in America*. New York: Harcourt, 2004. |
| Joseph Nicolosi and Linda Ames Nicolosi | *A Parent's Guide to Preventing Homosexuality*. Downer's Grove, IL: InterVarsity, 2002. |
| Benjie Nycum and Michael Glatze | *XY Survival Guide*. San Francisco: XY Publishing, 2000. |
| Charlotte J. Patterson and Anthony R. D'Augelli | *Lesbian, Gay, and Bisexual Identities and Youth: Psychological Perspectives*. Oxford: Oxford University Press, 2001. |
| Jonathan Rauch | *Gay Marriage: Why It Is Good for Gays, Good for Straights, and Good for America*. New York: Times Books, 2004. |
| Ritch C. Savin-Williams | *Mom, Dad, I'm Gay: How Families Negotiate Coming Out*. Washington, DC: American Psychological Association, 2001. |
| Alan Sears and Craig Osten | *The Homosexual Agenda: Exposing the Principal Threat to Religious Freedom Today*. Nashville, TN: Broadman and Holman, 2003. |
| Ralph R. Smith and Russel R. Windes | *Progay/Antigay: The Rhetorical War Over Sexuality*. Thousand Oaks, CA: Sage, 2000. |
| Judith E. Snow | *How It Feels to Have a Lesbian or Gay Parent: A Book by Kids for Kids of All Ages*. New York: Harrington Park, 2004. |
| Gretchen A. Stiers | *From This Day Forward: Commitment, Marriage, and Family in Lesbian and Gay Relationships*. New York: Palgrave Macmillan, 2000. |

| John R.W. Stott | *Same-Sex Partnerships?: A Christian Perspective.* New York: Fleming H. Revell, 1998. |
| David Strah and Susanna Margolis | *Gay Dads: A Celebration of Fatherhood.* Los Angeles: J.P. Tarcher, 2003. |
| Jeffrey Weeks, Brian Heaphy, and Catherine Donovan | *Same-Sex Intimacies: Families of Choice and Other Life Experiments.* New York: Routledge, 2001. |
| Bonnie Zimmerman | *Lesbian Histories and Cultures: An Encyclopedia.* New York: Garland, 2000. |

## Periodicals

| *Advocate* | "Our Readers Get Married," February 17, 2004. |
| Joshua K. Baker | "Summary of Opinion Research on Same-Sex Marriage," *iMAPP Policy Brief,* December 5, 2003. |
| Ginia Bellafante | "Two Fathers, with One Happy to Stay Home," *New York Times,* January 12, 2004. |
| Linda Bowles | "No Child Is Born to Be Homosexual," *Conservative Chronicle,* May 30, 2001. |
| Karen Breslau, Brad Stone, Debra Rosenberg, and Tamara Lipper | "Outlaw Vows," *Newsweek,* March 1, 2004. |
| Chris Bull | "What Makes a Mom," *Advocate,* November 25, 2003. |
| *Christianity Today* | "Let No Law Put Asunder," February 2004. |
| Victoria Clarke | "What About the Children? Arguments Against Lesbian and Gay Parenting," *Women's Studies International Forum,* September/October 2001. |
| Lynette Clemetson | "Both Sides Court Black Churches in the Battle over Gay Marriage," *New York Times,* March 1, 2004. |
| John Cloud | "The New Face of Gay Power," *Time,* October 13, 2003. |
| David Orgon Coolidge | "What the Vermont Court Has Wrought," *Weekly Standard,* January 17, 2000. |
| *CQ Researcher* | "Disputed Studies Give Gay Parents Good Marks," September 5, 2003. |
| Peggy Dresler | "Do Boys Need Daddies? The Moral Development of Sons of Lesbians," *In the Family,* Autumn 2000. |
| Lisa Duggan | "Holy Matrimony!" *Nation,* March 15, 2004. |
| *Economist* | "Out in Front," February 21, 2004. |
| Franklin Foer | "Marriage Counselor," *Atlantic Monthly,* March 2004. |
| Dan Gilgoff, Kenneth T. Walsh, Terence Samuel, and Justin Ewers | "Tied in Knots by Gay Marriage," *U.S. News & World Report,* March 8, 2004. |

| | |
|---|---|
| Erica Goode | "A Rainbow of Differences in Gays' Children," *New York Times*, July 17, 2001. |
| Thomas J. Gumbleton | "Yes, Gay Men Should Be Ordained," *America*, September 30, 2002. |
| Vicky Hallett | "Who Do You Love?" *U.S. News & World Report*, July 14, 2003. |
| Linda Harvey | "The World According to PFLAG: Why PFLAG and Children Don't Mix," *National Association for Research and Therapy of Homosexuality*, December 2002. |
| Doug Ireland | "Rebuilding the Gay Movement," *Nation*, July 12, 1999. |
| Toby Johnson | "The Evolution of Gay Consciousness," *Genre*, April 2000. |
| John W. Kennedy | "Gay Parenting on Trial," *Christianity Today*, July 8, 2002. |
| Stanley Kurtz | "Oh Canada! Will Gay Marriage Stand?" *National Review*, June 13, 2003. |
| Richard Lacayo | "For Better or For Worse?" *Time*, February 29, 2004. |
| Joseph Landau | "Misjudged: What *Lawrence* Hasn't Wrought," *New Republic*, February 16, 2004. |
| Jeni Loftus | "America's Liberalization in Attitudes Toward Homosexuality, 1973 to 1998," *American Sociological Review*, October 2001. |
| Rona Marech | "Devastating Side of Gay Liberation: Straight Spouse Network Eases Pain," *San Francisco Chronicle*, January 6, 2003. |
| *National Review* | "The Right Amendment," January 26, 2004. |
| Lisa Neff | "Gay in the Navy," *Advocate*, March 30, 2004. |
| George Neumayr | "Marriage on the Rocks," *American Spectator*, February 2004. |
| *The New American* | "UN Favors Homosexual Agenda," September 8, 2003. |
| *Newsweek* | "The War over Gay Marriage," July 7, 2003. |
| Dennis O'Brien | "A More Perfect Union," *Christian Century*, January 27, 2004. |
| Katherine A. O'Hanlan, Suzanne L. Dibble, H.J.J. Hagan, and Rachel Davids | "Advocacy for Women's Health Should Include Lesbian Health," *Journal of Women's Health*, March 2004. |
| John O'Sullivan | "The Bells Are Ringing . . ." *National Review*, March 8, 2004. |
| Mark E. Pietrzyk | "Pathology of the Ex-Gay Movement," *Gay & Lesbian Review*, Summer 2000. |
| Katha Pollitt | "Adam and Steve: Together at Last," *Nation*, December 15, 2003. |

| Robert Scheer | "Bush Plays Pope on Gay Marriage," *Nation*, August 18, 2003. |
|---|---|
| Nara Schoenberg | "Encouraged by Greater Tolerance, a Growing Number of Gay Teens Are Coming Out in High School," *Chicago Tribune*, May 12, 2003. |
| Scott Sherman | "Our Son Is Happy, What Else Matters?" *Newsweek*, September 16, 2002. |
| Glenn T. Stanton | "The Human Case Against Same-Sex Marriage," *CitizenLink*, December 27, 2003. |
| Andrew Sullivan | "Why the M Word Matters to Me," *Time*, February 16, 2004. |
| Michelle Tauber and Julie Jordan | "Sweet Harmony," *People*, February 23, 2004. |
| Chris Taylor | "I Do . . . No You Don't!" *Time*, March 1, 2004. |
| Jyoti Thottam | "Why Breaking Up Is So Hard to Do," *Time*, March 1, 2004. |
| *USA Today Magazine* | "Adoption More Open for Gays and Lesbians," April 2003. |
| David Usborne | "Gay with Children," *New York Magazine*, November 3, 2003. |
| Jacqueline Woodson | "Motherhood, My Way," *Essence*, December 2003. |
| Shawn Zeller | "Marching On, but Apart," *National Journal*, January 12, 2002. |

# INDEX